GRADE 3
Grammar and Writing Handbook

ISBN: 0–328–07539–6

4 5 6 7 8 9 10 V000 09 08 07 06 05

scottforesman.com

Editorial Offices: Glenview, Illinois • Parsippany, New Jersey • New York, New York
Sales Offices: Parsippany, New Jersey • Duluth, Georgia • Glenview, Illinois
Coppell, Texas • Ontario, California • Mesa, Arizona

TABLE OF CONTENTS

Writer's Guide 5

Grammar and Writing Lessons 23

Writer's Guide

Ideas and Content

Before you write, you need to have a **main idea** and a reason, or **purpose,** for writing. The main idea is the most important point you want to make. Your purpose may be to persuade, to inform, to describe, or just to entertain your readers.

A note to a friend has a main idea and a purpose.

Main Idea Convince a friend to see your new kitten

Purpose To persuade someone

Details Lively and interesting words, such as *fluffy, purr,* and *leap,* make word pictures for your reader. Details give important information.

> Jorge,
>   Come to my house tomorrow to see my new, fluffy kitten. She loves to purr and leap.
>   Avi

The birds are eating. (no details)
The gray pigeons peck at the dry bread.
   (details to show what is happening)

FOCUS

Stay on your topic and use only details that are about your main idea.

Strategies for Choosing a Main Idea and Purpose

- Choose something you know well or would like to learn about. Your topic could be your favorite aunt or the planets.
- Think about your purpose for writing. An adventure story would entertain. A how-to report would inform readers.

A Match the number of each sentence with the purpose that it fits best.

Ⓐ Inform Ⓑ Persuade Ⓒ Describe Ⓓ Entertain

1. Green plants help clean the air we breathe.
2. Let me tell you a funny story about my dad.
3. Doctor Jackson is tall and thin and has bright red hair.
4. Our school really needs a new gym.

B Some sentences below do not stay on the topic of the circus. Write the letters of those sentences.

A The wrinkly elephants swayed to the loud music.
B My new sandals were very comfortable.
C Three white poodles pranced around the ring.
D A jolly clown with fuzzy, orange hair juggled balls.
E Loreen and her mom went to the beach last week.
F The fierce lions leaped through fiery hoops.

C Choose one of the main-idea sentences below. Then write three sentences about the topic. Remember to use clear details.

- My best friend is an interesting person.
- I had an exciting adventure last month.
- Girls and boys can be good friends.

Organization

A careful writer tells about events and details in order. Your **organization** builds a frame to hold your writing. The frame keeps your ideas in place.

Here are some ways to organize your writing.

- a story with a beginning, middle, and end
- a comparison-contrast
- a description from top to bottom
- a how-to explanation

Before you write your first word, think about how you will build your writing. For example, if you want to tell what happened at a school meeting, you would write a report. If you want to explain how to ride a scooter, you would write a how-to explanation.

Once you decide on your frame, choose the details you want to include. You will also have to think about how to arrange your details from beginning to end.

Strategies for Organizing Ideas

- Begin with the most important detail or save it for last.
- Use order words such as *first, later,* and *last.*
- Put details that are alike in the same paragraph.

GRAPHIC ORGANIZER

A graphic organizer such as a chart, story map, or web can help you organize your ideas.

A Match the number of the topic with the letter of the kind of organization that works best.

1. Our green parakeet, Snuffles   **A** Comparison-contrast

2. How to make apple muffins   **B** Story

3. Car or train: which is better?   **C** Description

4. What happened on my vacation   **D** How-to explanation

B Choose a detail from the box to complete each sentence. Write the paragraph.

parrot	first pair of skates	new sweater
skating rink	read a book	library
slipped and fell	helped her up	started to cry

Marie's First Try

5. My cousin Marie bought her _____ last Monday. **6.** The next day, she went to the _____. **7.** As she stepped onto the ice, Marie _____. **8.** She wasn't hurt, but she _____. **9.** We skated over to her and _____.

C Think of a time when you learned something new. Tell how you learned each step. Use order words such as *first, then,* and *next* to organize the details.

Voice

Your writing shows your special style and personality. Use your writer's **voice** to shape your writing. A writer's voice may be funny or serious. It could be friendly or formal. When your writing voice is strong and clear, readers believe what you have to say.

- I was so tired that I got into bed early. (weak voice)
- I was so worn out that I crawled into bed an hour before dinnertime. I didn't wake up until Dad shouted that breakfast was ready. (strong voice)

Strategies for Developing a Writer's Voice

- Think about your readers and about your reason for writing. Use a light, friendly voice when you write a letter to a cousin or when you tell a funny story. Use a more serious voice for a book report or for directions.
- Your choice of words should match your voice. In informal writing, you might use contractions or slang to make your writing sound like your everyday voice. A letter to the editor of your school newspaper would have a more serious voice.
- Use your writer's voice to speak directly to your audience. If your voice is strong, readers want to keep on reading.

> **VOICE**
>
> **Try reading your work aloud to see if your writing sounds like *you*. If it doesn't, think about what might be missing from it.**

A Match each opening sentence with the letter of the reader it fits best.

    A Aunt Kira in Texas   **C** The school principal
    B The head zookeeper   **D** A group of classmates

1. We would like another microscope for the science room.
2. Thanks for that great new game you sent me.
3. May we please have a special tour of the jungle exhibit?
4. Let's throw a party for Miss Peters!

B Read each sentence. Write **E** if you would use an everyday voice in your writing. Write **S** if you would use a serious voice.

5. You are writing to the editor of the local newspaper.
6. You are writing a note to your best friend.
7. You are writing an e-mail message to your cousin.
8. You are writing a report about sea turtles.

C Choose one of the following opening sentences. Add sentences to write a paragraph about the topic. Use a voice that fits the main idea and the audience.

- Would you like to make a bowl of cereal?
- Dear Editor, The schoolyard needs some new paint.
- Spring and fall are my favorite seasons, but for different reasons.

Word Choice

Words are the writer's handiest tool. Build your writing with exact nouns, strong verbs, and vivid adjectives. Your style will be interesting and lively.

- I like the bakery because it smells good. (dull and plain)
- The bakery smells like sweet cinnamon rolls and fresh, crusty bread. (lively and detailed)

Strategies for Choosing the Right Words

- Choose exact nouns. (*spaniel* instead of *dog, broccoli* instead of *vegetable)*
- Use strong verbs. (*shatter* instead of *break, shriek* instead of *yell)*
- Replace dull words such as *nice, bad,* and *thing* with clear words. ("The owner was greedy and cruel" instead of "The owner was bad.")
- Include words that use our senses. ("The sun was as warm as a blanket" instead of "The sun was warm.")
- Don't be wordy. (*suddenly* instead of "with great suddenness")
- Include specific details. ("Dan slurped up soup and ate crackers" instead of "Dan was a noisy eater.")

> **WORDS WITH PEP**
>
> **When you want to spice up your writing, think about exciting words such as *sparkle, zoom, velvety,* and *lumpy.***

A Replace the underlined words with more exact words from the box. Write the paragraph.

delicious	stirs	onions and garlic
dips	beams	bubbles and steams

1. The cook <u>makes</u> the spicy soup. 2. The kitchen smells like <u>food</u>. 3. She <u>puts</u> her finger into the pot for a taste. 4. The soup <u>is hot.</u> 5. The cook <u>smiles</u> and nods. 6. Her meals are always <u>good.</u>

B Change each underlined word to a more vivid word of your own. Write the sentences.

7. Jeff and Pooch <u>went</u> through the park.
8. It was a <u>nice</u> autumn day.
9. Then Pooch <u>saw</u> something in the grass.
10. He <u>went</u> across the park.
11. The little squirrel was <u>fast.</u>
12. It <u>went</u> up a tree.
13. Pooch <u>looked</u> sadly at the tree.
14. The squirrel had <u>gone!</u>

C Write a description of an animal you have seen. Use strong, vivid words to make your writing come alive.

Sentences

Good writing has a natural flow. Different kinds of **sentences** should make it sound smooth and clear. When you hear a story read aloud, listen to the style and the rhythm of the sentences.

Here are some ways to improve your sentences.

- Use different kinds of sentences. Questions, commands, and exclamations add style to your writing.
- Make sure your sentences are not all short and choppy. Sometimes a longer sentence helps the writing flow.
- Use different beginnings. Starting too many sentences with *I, she, the,* or *a* can be boring.
- Use connecting words. Words such as *even though, because, while,* and *so* can join sentences to make them more interesting to read.

Strategy for Improving Your Sentences

Read a piece of your writing. Each time you start a sentence with *I, she, the,* or *a,* circle the word. Underline all the short, choppy sentences. See how many different kinds of sentences you use.

Write this information on scratch paper. Then see which things you can change to make the writing better. Have you used too many statements instead of other kinds of sentences? Are most of your sentences short and choppy? Keep this information in a writing folder to help you improve your writing.

A Use the connecting words in ( ) to join the two sentences. Write the sentences.

1. We went to the seashore. We could splash in the waves. (so)
2. Hal loves the winter. Our state has tons of snow. (even though)
3. Our kitten meowed loudly. I got her food ready. (while)
4. The dog needed a bath. He had rolled in the mud. (because)

B Rearrange the words in sentences **6.–9.** so that *I* is not the first word. Start with the underlined phrase.

Example: I jumped out of bed <u>this morning</u>.
Answer: This morning I jumped out of bed.

5. I could not find one brown sock. 6. I searched everywhere <u>before breakfast.</u> 7. I caught the school bus <u>just in time.</u> 8. I opened my lunchbox <u>at noon.</u> 9. I found the sock <u>on top of my sandwich!</u>

C Write a short story about finding something that you thought you had lost. Use different kinds of sentences. Be sure to start your sentences with different words.

Conventions

Conventions are rules for writing. Capital letters show where a sentence begins. A period, question mark, or exclamation mark signals the end of a sentence. A new paragraph begins with an indentation. Grammar and spelling follow patterns.

- joe asted his techur for a pensul then he could gets to work. (weak conventions)
- Joe asked his teacher for a pencil. Then he could get to work. (strong conventions)

Strategies for Conventions of Writing

- Start sentences with a capital letter and end with a punctuation mark.
- Make sure each sentence tells a complete idea. Each subject and verb should agree.
- Don't change verb tenses without a good reason.
- Be sure special names are capitalized correctly.
- Check for correct punctuation. Follow rules for commas, apostrophes, and other punctuation marks.
- Use a dictionary or spell-checker for difficult words.

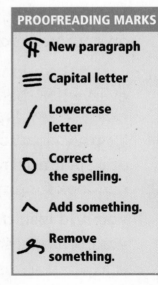

PROOFREADING MARKS

¶	New paragraph
≡	Capital letter
/	Lowercase letter
○	Correct the spelling.
∧	Add something.
℘	Remove something.

A Choose the correct word in ( ) to complete each sentence. Write the sentences.

1. Winter (is, are) my favorite time of year.
2. My family and (us, I) love to sled and throw snowballs.
3. We certainly (enjoy, enjoying) the cold.
4. I have (took, taken) my friends skiing too.
5. They all (likes, like) winter sports a lot.

B Look at each sentence. Correct any mistakes in punctuation, grammar, and spelling. Write the paragraph.

   6. The united states is a large country. 7. Have you seen our land from coast to coast. 8. Mountains and valleys is in almost every state. 9. Swimers and boaters enjoy the lakes and rivers. 10. try to see some part of our wonderful country on your next vacation.

C Write three sentences about one of the topics below. Remember to follow the rules for capitalization, punctuation, grammar, and spelling. Trade papers with a classmate and look for anything that should be changed.

- A sport I would like to learn
- A trip I would like to take
- A job that seems interesting

> **PROOFREADING**
>
> When you proof-read, look carefully for mistakes. Use a ruler to check each line from start to finish. Read aloud to catch errors.

Using a Scoring Rubric

What makes a piece of writing *excellent?* When is writing *good,* or *not good?* One way to judge a piece of writing is to use a scoring **rubric.** A rubric is a checklist of *qualities,* or things to look for. See pages 6–17 for a discussion of these qualities.

Rubrics give a number score for each thing you are looking for. You can use a rubric such as the one below to judge your writing.

SCORE	IDEAS/CONTENT	ORGANIZATION	VOICE	WORD CHOICE	SENTENCES	CONVENTIONS
4	Clear, focused, well-supported ideas	Smooth flow of ideas from beginning to end, with connecting words	Honest, engaging, lively writing	Precise, interesting, and accurate words	Smooth, varied, and rhythmic sentences	Excellent control with only minor errors
3	Ideas usually focused and supported	Information given in some order	At times reveals writer's personality	Correct and adequate words	Generally smooth, varied sentences	Good control; no serious errors prevent understanding
2	Ideas sometimes unfocused and undeveloped	Little direction from beginning to end	Fails to engage audience or show emotion	Limited vocabulary; lacks freshness	Awkward or wordy sentences with little variety	Weak control with errors that make writing hard to read
1	Ideas confusing and unsupported	Ideas hard to follow with no direction	Flat writing with no feeling	Incorrect, dull, or overused words	Choppy sentences; run-ons or fragments; *and* overused as connector	Many errors that prevent understanding

Following are four responses to a prompt. Read each response and the notes below it. This will show how each piece got its score.

Writing Prompt: Write about a time when someone helped you feel better or you helped someone else feel better.

One day I got the flu. I was sick to my stomack and felt really dizzy. Then my dad said to lie down. Next, he brought me ginger ale with a twisty straw. Finally, my stomack stopped aching. My parents and my brother had helped me feel better.

Then everybody else got sick! Even the dog was droopy! I carried up ginger ale on a fancy tray. I hope we never get sick like this again.

Score 4
Ideas/Content Focused and supported by many details
Organization Order words *then, next,* and *finally* move story along; has a clear ending
Voice Strongly engages readers ("Even the dog was droopy!")
Word Choice Vivid word choice and images (*twisty, fancy tray*)
Sentences Clear, smooth sentences
Conventions Few mistakes; a misspelling (*stomack*)

One day I helped my next-door naybor clean up his backyard. We raked and put leaves in blue bags to recycle them. Then we sawed some branches off the tree that was leening against his house. My help made him feel better because his wife just passd away. The next day I went back to bring him a piece of cake and a little card I made. He said, "Matthew, you are like a grandkid." that made me feel good.

Score 3

Ideas/Content Focused on the idea of making someone feel better and supported with details *(blue bags, piece of cake, little card)*

Organization Story has a beginning, middle, and end; order words to make order of events clear

Voice Expresses feelings ("that made me feel good")

Word Choice Good use of verbs *(raked, sawed);* exact nouns *(leaves, branches)*

Sentences Varied and smooth sentences

Conventions Some mistakes; some spelling errors *(naybor, leening, passd);* a capitalization error ("that made me feel good.")

Someone made me feel better when I busted my head. And my mom made me feel better. They took me to the hospitil. And they bought me a toy and it made me feel better. And the next day they brought me more stuff and they bought me moovies and games. And then at 8:00 I fell asleep. And in the morning I feel a little better. I'm never going to do that again.

Score 2

Ideas/Content Focused on the idea of someone who is helped to feel better, but needs more details

Organization Moves from a beginning to an end

Voice Gives reader a sense of who the writer is

Word Choice Many dull or repeated words (*took, stuff, feel*)

Sentences Opening not very clear; too many choppy sentences; most sentences begin with *And*

Conventions Misspellings (*hospitil, moovies*); change in verb tense ("I feel a little better"); grammar error (*busted*)

> My mom halp me when I am skare. She trn on the
> Light so I whent Be skare all night.

Score 1

Ideas/Content Main idea not supported by details

Organization Time order not clear

Voice Writer not involved

Word Choice Dull word choice

Sentences Sentences difficult to understand

Conventions Incorrect capitalization *(Light, Be);* misspellings *(halp, skare, trn, whent);* incorrect use of verb tense and form *(halp, trn)*

Grammar and Writing Lessons

Sentences

A **sentence** is a group of words that tells a complete thought. A group of words that does not tell a complete thought is called a **fragment.** In a sentence, the words are in an order that makes sense. All sentences begin with a capital letter and end with a punctuation mark.

Sentence: I enjoy vacations with my family.
Not a sentence: Enjoy vacations with my family.

A Read each group of words. Write the one in each pair that is a sentence.

1. Do you like to be outdoors during warm weather?
No coats or scarves.
2. Wearing shorts and T-shirts.
Summer is great for hiking and swimming.
3. We plan to climb a mountain on this trip.
Plenty of exercise!
4. It is almost three thousand miles from my home.
Will have an exciting trip.

Read this story. Write the three complete sentences.

5. The mountain rises high in the sky. **6.** Older than the forest. **7.** Few people have climbed to the top. **8.** Snow never melts at the top of the mountain. **9.** Stories about climbers.

B Read each group of words. Write **S** if the group of words is a sentence. Write **NS** if the group of words is not a sentence.

1. My sister wanted to go to the beach.
2. Had been to the beach many times.
3. Dad solved the problem for us.
4. We could see mountains and the Pacific Ocean.
5. Everybody in the family!
6. Packed for the trip last night.
7. I traveled by airplane for the first time.
8. Had a book about Washington State.
9. Can't wait.
10. This will be the best vacation ever!

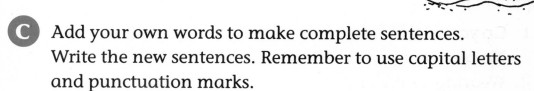

C Add your own words to make complete sentences. Write the new sentences. Remember to use capital letters and punctuation marks.

11. _____ go to the beach
12. My friends and I _____
13. _____ jumped into the icy water
14. We _____
15. _____ rest in the warm sunlight
16. After my rest, I _____
17. _____ look for seashells
18. _____ love the sound of the water
19. My family _____

Review and Assess

Read each group of words. Write **S** if it is a sentence.
Write **NS** if it is not a sentence.

1. You can take a vacation right where you live.
2. Pretend that you have never seen this place.
3. For a walk around your town.
4. May see your town in a new way.
5. List of questions and find out the answers.
6. The library is a good place to start.

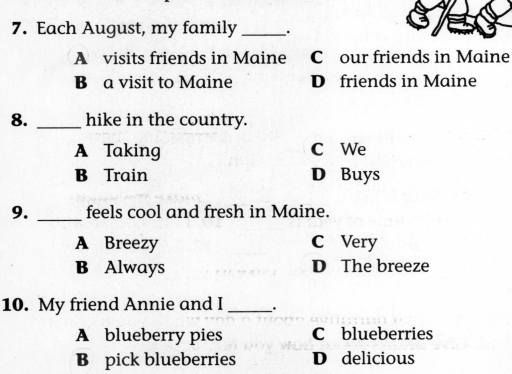

Write the letter of the word or group of
words that will complete each sentence.

7. Each August, my family _____.

   A visits friends in Maine   **C** our friends in Maine
   B a visit to Maine   **D** friends in Maine

8. _____ hike in the country.

   A Taking   **C** We
   B Train   **D** Buys

9. _____ feels cool and fresh in Maine.

   A Breezy   **C** Very
   B Always   **D** The breeze

10. My friend Annie and I _____.

    A blueberry pies   **C** blueberries
    B pick blueberries   **D** delicious

Telling About *You* in Personal Narratives

A personal narrative shares something important or exciting that happened to you. Your narrative should include sentences that tell the reader how you felt, acted, and looked at the time.

A Complete the sentences below with details from the list.

girl in green goggles   waved at me
was splashing in the waves   shy and embarrassed
my sister's baggy swimsuit   comfortable all at once

1. One day, I _____.
2. Up from the water popped a _____.
3. Oh, no, I was wearing _____!
4. My red face showed I was _____.
5. Suddenly, the girl smiled and _____.
6. Then I felt _____.

B Create a word picture of yourself by completing these sentences. Write the new paragraph.

7. My hair is like a _____. 8. _____ make me laugh. 9. My favorite time of year is _____. 10. I like people who _____. 11. I am really good at _____. 12. My friends say that I _____. 13. After school, I like to _____.

C Write a personal narrative about a day when you met a new friend. Give details about how you felt, acted, and looked.

Subjects and Predicates

The **subject** is the part of the sentence that tells whom or what the sentence is about. All the words in the subject are called the **complete subject.**

Complete Subject

The excited girl picked beautiful flowers.

The **predicate** is the part of the sentence that tells something about the subject. All the words in the predicate are called the **complete predicate.**

Complete Predicate

The excited girl 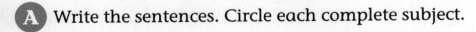 picked beautiful flowers.

A Write the sentences. Circle each complete subject.

1. Lonely Cinderella visits the three pigs.
2. They bake oatmeal cookies.
3. The hungry girl eats all the cookies.
4. The smallest pig makes some more cookies.

Write the sentences. Underline each complete predicate.

5. Silly Pinocchio plays in the forest.
6. A thunderstorm scares him.
7. The little boy runs into a nearby house.
8. Sleepy Goldilocks naps in the smallest bed.

B Write the sentences. Circle the complete predicate.

1. The tiny hummingbird flies onto the branch.
2. Its bright wings flap quickly.
3. The thin branch has lovely flowers.
4. Each blossom is filled with tasty pollen.
5. The bird's long beak picks out the pollen.
6. Its tongue is made for catching small bugs.
7. A ladybug passes by.
8. The bird gobbles up the ladybug.
9. A hummingbird's day is spent gathering food.

C Match a subject to a predicate so that each complete sentence makes sense. Write the sentences.

Subjects	Predicates
10. Fairy tales	reads that story.
11. Many readers	are fun to read.
12. My favorite story	are delighted by the tales.
13. Goldilocks	is your favorite story?
14. He	annoyed the three bears.
15. What	is "Goldilocks and the Three Bears."

Review and Assess

Write the sentences. Circle the complete subject.
Draw a line under the complete predicate.

1. My younger brother dreamed about flying.
2. Little Arthur made a pair of wings.
3. The neighbors watched him flap around the yard.
4. His best friend just shook his head.
5. Silly Arthur still flapped his wings.
6. He believed in his dreams.

Write the letter of the subject or predicate
that completes the sentence and makes sense.

7. Uncle Harry _____.

   A my favorite person   **C** lucky
   B has a telescope   **D** each day

8. _____ begged to look through the telescope.

   A Everyone   **C** Telescope
   B Got excited **D** Opened the box

9. Cousin Sue _____.

   A took the first look   **C** the fastest runner
   B the oldest child   **D** a tune

10. _____ helps us see the stars and planets.

   A Unfolds   **C** Works
   B A telescope **D** Looks

Adding Details to Subjects and Predicates

Interesting sentences hold a reader's attention. The details in your subjects and predicates tell your reader what is happening.

- Squirrels and a chipmunk ate.
- Two squirrels and a noisy chipmunk ate in the garden.

A Choose details from the list below and add them to the subject or predicate in each sentence. Write the new sentences.

crunchy	graceful	leafy
on the fence	chirping	from my window

1. Today, I closely watched nature _____. **2.** The _____ oak tree shaded the lawn. **3.** A frisky squirrel ate the _____ acorns. **4.** A _____ blackbird came to the bird feeder. **5.** A _____ cat slipped through the fence. **6.** Colorful butterflies landed _____.

B Think of a real or imaginary dream. Add details that will hold a reader's interest. Write the new sentences.

7. Once I dreamed about _____.
8. This strange dream took place in _____.
9. I met an animal that had _____.
10. I felt _____.
11. The dream ended when _____.

C Write a short personal narrative about a time when you were lost. Add details to your subjects and predicates.

Statements and Questions

A **statement** is a sentence that tells something. It ends with a period. A **question** is a sentence that asks something. It ends with a question mark.

Statement: Animals can help us in many ways.
Question: How did people first train animals?

A Read the sentences. Write **statement** or **question** after each sentence.

1. Long ago, all animals were wild.
2. Which animals became pets?
3. Dogs could be trained.
4. How did dogs and people become friends?
5. People fed the dogs and cared for them.
6. Today, many people choose dogs as pets.

Write each sentence with the correct punctuation mark.

7. Other animals are used for food and work
8. What food do we get from cows
9. Cows give us milk and beef
10. What kind of work can animals do
11. Horses and oxen can pull wagons
12. Do dogs have special jobs
13. Dogs can guard homes and herd sheep
14. Have you ever heard of a cat with a job

B Write only the sentences that are questions. Add the correct punctuation mark to the sentence.

1. Do you know how to train a dog
2. I took a class all about dog training
3. What do you think helped Roxie to learn
4. Do you want to know about dog training
5. The trainer starts with tasty treats for the dog
6. When Roxie obeyed an order, she was fed
7. What is the first thing a dog learns
8. May I show you some of Roxie's tricks

C Add one of the words from the box to turn each statement into a question. Write the new sentences. Use correct capitalization and punctuation. You can use a word more than once.

do	would	can	will

9. Yolanda and Paul take riding lessons.
10. You join them for a lesson today.
11. The twins enjoy riding western style.
12. You climb up without any help.
13. You like a gentle horse for your first ride.
14. Yolanda and Paul ride for an hour this afternoon.

Review and Assess

Write the sentences. Add the correct end punctuation. Write **S** for a statement and **Q** for a question.

1. My first visit to a ranch was exciting
2. The owner of the ranch was a real cowboy
3. Would you like to see pictures of the ranch
4. Do you know who that girl on the horse is
5. The horse seemed very big to me
6. Can I show you a picture of my favorite cowgirl

Write the letter of the sentence that is written correctly.

7. **A** What is your story about
   B I will write a letter
   C Did you take pictures?
   D This is my pony

8. **A** I collect shells.
   B is the shell cracked?
   C Are these conch shells
   D Tell me about it?

9. **A** I want to be a chef
   B this is good pastry.
   C baking is my hobby?
   D Did you bake that cake?

10. **A** Do you sing well
    B You have real talent
    C We will sing a song.
    D let's sing some more?

Writing Statements and Questions

Good writers use different types of sentences to tell a story. Using questions can help you tell your story in a lively way.

- Davy plans to travel through time. He wants to build a spaceship. Can he do it? "Don't be silly," people tell him.

A All of the sentences in the personal narrative below are statements. Rewrite the underlined sentences as questions to make the paragraph more interesting.

1. I can build a time-travel machine. **2.** It will be something I finish all by myself. **3.** There is enough wood to build my machine. **4.** It's a good idea to plan these things first. **5.** I should ask my dad if I can borrow his old tool kit. **6.** I will promise to be careful.

B Write your own questions to complete this personal narrative.

_____? I learned to paint with watercolors yesterday. At first, the colors seemed too light. Then I saw that I had too much water on my brush. The art teacher showed me what to do. I took a fresh piece of paper. Before I started over, I took a deep breath. _____?

C Write a short personal narrative about something a friend or family member helped you do. Use questions to make your story more exciting.

Writing a Personal Narrative Anthony Reynoso ... **35**

Commands and Exclamations

A **command** is a sentence that tells someone to do something. It ends with a period. An **exclamation** is a sentence that shows strong feelings, such as anger, surprise, fear, or excitement. It ends with an exclamation mark.

Command: Cover your mouth when you cough.
Exclamation: How sick I feel!

A Write **C** if the sentence is a command. Write **E** if the sentence is an exclamation.

1. Get ready for a visit to the doctor. C
2. What a bad cough you have! E
3. Please let the doctor check your throat. C
4. How red your throat looks! E
5. Take a deep breath for the doctor. C

Write each sentence. Add the correct end punctuation.

6. Give Cindy this basket of oranges
7. How juicy this fruit is
8. Please tell her I will visit her tomorrow
9. Wow, I am so happy to see you
10. Bring her some flowers too

B Write each sentence and add a period or an exclamation mark. Then write **C** for a command or **E** for an exclamation.

1. Remember these health rules
2. Wash your hands before eating
3. You will love these vegetables
4. Eat three servings of vegetables a day
5. What tasty green beans you cooked, Mom
6. How healthy we will be
7. Take your vitamins
8. What a lot of energy I have every morning

C Add a word from the box to complete each command or exclamation. Write the new sentences, using correct end punctuation.

Look	Throw	Wow
Learn	Grab	Teach

9. _____ about this new game
10. _____ me how to play the game
11. _____ a soccer ball off the shelf
12. _____ it past that tree
13. _____ , you can do that really well
14. _____ for the lost ball with me

Review and Assess

Write each sentence, using the correct end punctuation.
Then write **C** for a command or **E** for an exclamation.

1. Try to make some new friends this year
2. I don't want any new friends
3. I love my old friends
4. Talk to different classmates each day
5. Ask them what they like to do
6. Yes, I like that new girl a lot

Write the letter of the answer that best completes
the type of sentence in ( ).

7. Julie is my best _____ (exclamation)

    A friend?   **C** friend!

    B Friend.   **D** friend.

8. _____ meet me at the zoo. (command)

    A Please   **C** Please!

    B please   **D** please!

9. That's a great place to _____ (exclamation)

    A Go!   **C** Go.

    B go!   **D** go.

10. _____ to the zoo one day soon, please. (command)

    A take me   **C** take me.

    B Take me!   **D** Take me

Making Your Narrative Lively

You can make your story lively and exciting for your reader by using different kinds of sentences. Commands and exclamations tell how you feel.

- Start writing your song today.
- How excited we are about the contest!

A Add words to complete these exclamations.

1. Don't forget to enter the songwriting contest. **2.** What a great song you _____! **3.** Please play that fantastic melody. **4.** Sit down and listen closely. **5.** What a catchy _____! **6.** You should be a songwriter. **7.** Wow, you're a great _____ too!

B Change the two underlined sentences to commands in this personal narrative. Then finish the paragraph with an exclamation for a strong ending.

8. There's an art show at my school this week. **9.** I hope you don't forget to come. **10.** I wish you would look at my drawings first. **11.** One day, I might be an artist. **12.** I think you will enjoy the paintings and pottery. **13.** _____!

C Write a letter to a friend about a time when you tried your best to do something. Use commands and exclamations to make your writing lively.

Clear and Interesting Subjects

The subject of a sentence tells whom or what the sentence is about. The **simple subject** is the main noun or pronoun in the **complete subject.** Use subjects that give your readers clear information and that interest your audience.

- <u>I</u> love to run around the park.
- <u>My good friend, Caitlin, and I</u> run every day.

A One of the underlined words in each sentence is the simple subject. Write that word.

1. <u>The girls in my class</u> love sports.
2. <u>Our favorite teacher</u> plays soccer and hockey.
3. <u>The most popular sport</u> is probably baseball.
4. <u>A perfect day</u> would be six hours of gym class.

Write the sentence in each pair with the subject that is clearer.

5. <u>Darcy</u> throws a fast curve ball.
   <u>Our best pitcher, Darcy,</u> throws a fast curve ball.
6. <u>A seven-year-old named Vanessa</u> steps up to the plate.
   <u>Vanessa</u> steps up to the plate.
7. <u>Everybody</u> cheers for her.
   <u>Other team members</u> cheer for her.

B Write the complete subject in each sentence.

1. Mr. Wilson, our camp leader, taught us how to sew.
2. Some grumbling campers did not want to sew.
3. My cousin David didn't like sewing.
4. A boy in a red T-shirt wanted to swim.
5. Our teacher did not make them sew that first day.
6. The sewing project was making a quilt.
7. Both boys enjoyed working on the quilt.
8. Their strong fingers could move the needles well.

C Choose a clear and interesting subject from the box to complete each sentence. Write the sentences.

> My favorite place for concerts
> The students in my singing group
> Our summer outdoor concerts
> Some concert halls
> The woman with a beautiful voice

9. _____ perform for people all over.
10. _____ often sings at concerts.
11. _____ is the town hall.
12. _____ have seats for five hundred people!
13. _____ are fun for everyone.

Review and Assess

Write the sentences. Underline the complete subject
in each sentence.

1. My two friends, Derek and Jim, had a secret wish.
2. The bored boys wanted a circus to come to their town.
3. An amazing thing happened that very morning.
4. A clown on stilts strutted down Main Street.
5. A huge, wrinkled elephant marched behind him.
6. The surprised children couldn't believe their eyes.

Write the letter of the group of words that could
make the subject of each sentence clearer.

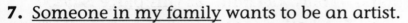

7. Someone in my family wants to be an artist.

    A A child named   **C** My older sister

    B Someone else   **D** Some girl

8. A school would be perfect for her.

    A School   **C** Some class

    B Anyplace   **D** An art school

9. A person at school wants to help my sister.

    A Miss Rice, a teacher,   **C** A friend

    B That woman   **D** A nice woman

10. Her things are really very good.

    A The pictures   **C** Her bright watercolors

    B Paintings   **D** Drawings and stuff

Using Details to Make Subjects Clear

Adding important details to the subject will make your writing clear and more interesting to the reader. Details help you tell your story.

- Some children are playing hopscotch.
- Three little girls with ponytails are playing hopscotch.

A Replace the underlined words with clear subjects from the list. Write the new sentences.

The way to play kickball	A strong player
This large, sunny yard	A big rubber ball
The best part of the game	My classmates and I

1. <u>We</u> are going to play kickball. **2.** <u>This place</u> is good for playing games. **3.** <u>A ball</u> is easy to kick too. **4.** <u>Something good</u> is that many people can play. **5.** <u>The thing to do</u> is to kick the ball to the bases. **6.** <u>A person</u> can kick a home run.

B Replace the underlined words with more interesting details of your own. Write the new sentences.

7. <u>One day</u>, we played an exciting game. **8.** <u>It</u> has just a few rules. **9.** <u>A family member</u> taught me this game. **10.** <u>We</u> taught my classmates how to play. **11.** <u>Other children</u> couldn't wait for me to teach them too!

C Write a personal narrative that tells about a good time you had with your friends. Include details to make the story come alive.

Writing a Personal Narrative

A **test** may ask you to write a personal narrative. Your narrative needs to have a beginning, a middle, and an end. Use time-order words such as *then* and *after*. Follow the tips below.

Understand the prompt. Make sure you know what to do. Read the prompt. A prompt for a personal narrative could look like this:

> **Write a personal narrative about a really interesting or exciting event from your own life. Be sure to choose just one experience or event to write about. Consider creating a mood of suspense or humor.**

Key phrases are *personal narrative, your own life,* and *experience or event.*

Find a good topic. Choose an important event that you remember well. Think about the details you want to include.

Organize your ideas. Make a story organizer like this:

Event Selling orange juice **When?** Last Saturday **Where?** In front of my house
1. We set up the stand with a table, a chair, cups, and a colorful sign. 2. We made fresh orange juice in Mom's juicer. 3. I put pitchers of orange juice on the table. 4. We earned $5.00.

Write a good beginning. An exciting topic sentence will make your audience want to read more.

Develop and elaborate ideas. Use information from your story organizer. Include words that show time, such as *later*.

Write a strong ending. The end of your story can be exciting.

Check your work. Reread your work and make any changes.

See how the story below answers the prompt, has a clear beginning, middle, and end, and uses time-order words.

My Juicy Business

1 — Last Saturday, I found out how to run a business.

2 — First, my sister and I made fresh orange juice in Mom's juicer.
Boy, did that juicer make the job easy! — 3

Later, we borrowed some fancy pitchers and — 4
a tablecloth from Grandma. We set up the stand with a
table, a chair, cups, and a colorful sign. Then we just had
to wait for the customers to stroll by. We had six customers in the first hour. At the end of the day, we had
earned $5.00. I guess even a kid can own a business. — 5

1. The first sentence organizes the whole story.
2. Time-order words show the sequence of events.
3. An exclamatory sentence adds interest.
4. Vivid details help readers picture the scene.
5. The strong ending shows the writer's personality.

Nouns

A **noun** names a person, a place, or a thing.

Person: My <u>aunt</u> is a <u>doctor</u>.
Places: She works at a <u>hospital</u> in a big <u>city</u>.
Things: She travels by <u>bus</u> to her <u>job</u>.

A One of the underlined words in each sentence is a noun. Write the noun.

1. <u>Starfish</u> live in oceans all <u>over</u> the world.
2. Most starfish <u>have</u> five <u>arms</u>.
3. These <u>animals</u> can be <u>tiny</u> or large.
4. Can a starfish <u>change</u> its <u>color</u>?
5. The <u>aquarium</u> has <u>many</u> starfish.

Each sentence has two nouns. One noun is underlined. Write the other noun.

6. The <u>starfish</u> has little spines.
7. This <u>creature</u> also has sticky feet.
8. They stick to rocks in the <u>water</u>.
9. Its enemies cannot pull the <u>starfish</u> off.
10. The <u>starfish</u> eats smaller animals all at once!
11. It pushes its <u>stomach</u> outside its body.
12. Do other <u>animals</u> eat food like this?

B Write the three nouns in each sentence.

1. A marsh is a home to many animals.
2. Have you seen the otter in the reeds and grass?
3. My brother found a cattail in the water.
4. This plant had a fuzzy top and a long stem.
5. My book has a picture of a muskrat.
6. Look at that red spot on the wing of that blackbird!
7. Birds, crabs, and clams all live here.
8. This wetland protects ponds and rivers.
9. My class started a project about swamps.
10. Reptiles hide in the grass and the trees.

C Add a noun from the box that makes sense to complete each sentence. Write the sentences.

beach	shells	waves	mosquito
food	seagulls	sand	

11. You will see many animals at the _____. 12. Some _____ wash crabs up onto the shore. 13. Their _____ crunch under your feet. 14. _____ fly over the water. 15. Are they hunting for _____ in the water? 16. Insects scurry through the grainy _____. 17. Be careful that a _____ doesn't bite you.

Review and Assess

Write the sentences. Underline all the nouns in each sentence.

1. Our family went for a hike in the woods.
2. My sister found purple flowers in the moss.
3. Many plants and animals live in the forest.
4. Did you hear about the raccoon, the deer, and the skunk?
5. Tall trees gave shade and shelter.
6. Chirping sounds came from a nest in the branches.

Read each sentence. Write the letter of
the word that is a noun.

7. I find a small, sparkling stream.

    A find   **C** small
    B stream   **D** sparkling

8. I am hunting for newts.

    A for   **C** newts
    B hunting   **D** am

9. Would you like to be my helper?

    A like   **C** be
    B helper   **D** Would

10. Start by cupping your hands like this.

    A hands   **C** by
    B your   **D** Start

Using Exact Nouns in Descriptions

Your description should include exact nouns that show *who,* *what,* and *where* to give your audience the whole picture.

- **Good:** Some <u>people</u> like to study <u>things</u>.
- **Better:** Some <u>students</u> like to study <u>insects</u>.

A Replace each underlined noun with a more exact noun from the list. Write the new paragraph.

> thread   T-shirt   sparrows   web   spiders

1. We are studying <u>bugs</u>. **2.** The spider spins its own cozy <u>home</u>. **3.** It travels on a thin, sticky <u>line</u>. **4.** Some spiders are the size of <u>birds</u>. **5.** I screamed when I found a spider on my <u>clothes</u>!

B Complete each sentence with an exact noun of your own. Write the sentences.

6. The strange animal sat in the _____.
7. His fuzzy head had three _____.
8. I brought him a piece of _____.
9. He ate it with a _____.
10. He thanked me with a _____.

C Write a postcard to a friend that describes an interesting animal you have seen at the zoo, in a book, or on television. Use exact nouns to give your friend a picture of what you saw.

Nouns in Sentences

A **noun** can be the main word in the subject of a sentence.
Nouns can also appear in other parts of a sentence.

> **Noun in the subject:** The gentle <u>king</u> welcomed Eric.
> **Noun in the predicate:** Eric found the missing <u>stone</u>.

A The complete subject of each sentence is underlined.
Write the noun that is the simple subject of each sentence.

1. <u>The surprised boy</u> woke up in a strange bed.
2. <u>Soft light</u> came in through the window.
3. <u>A scaly dragon</u> slept at the foot of the bed.
4. <u>This day</u> would be very different for Eric.

Write the sentences. Underline the noun
in each subject. Circle the nouns in each
predicate.

5. This <u>castle</u> was not his home in the city!
6. The <u>boy</u> crept out of bed and went down the stairs.
7. The dark <u>hall</u> led to a huge room with a big door.
8. A sad old <u>man</u> sat on a big chair in the corner.

B Choose the correct noun in ( ) to complete each sentence. Write the noun. Write **S** if the noun is in the subject. Write **P** if the noun is in the predicate.

1. A (king, robe) with a crooked crown sat on the throne.
2. The crown was missing a (room, jewel) from its center.
3. The king told the (throne, boy) about this problem.
4. A (thief, pen) had stolen the stone!
5. Eric listened to the king tell his (story, apple).
6. Then the thoughtful (boy, chair) explained his idea.
7. The king listened with a frown on his (foot, face).
8. Other (people, boy) in the kingdom had the same plan.
9. Would the (boy, crown) solve the problem?

C Write the sentences. Draw a line under the noun or nouns that are not part of the subject.

10. Eric promised to find the stolen jewel.
11. He went to his room to wake the dragon.
12. The sleepy dragon sneezed and blew his nose loudly.
13. Then the stone flew out of his mouth!
14. Eric smiled and went to find the king.
15. The happy king put the stone back in the crown.

Review and Assess

One part of each sentence is underlined.
Write the noun or nouns in that group of words.

1. I <u>want to travel to the moon</u>.
2. <u>My heroes</u> are all astronauts.
3. <u>These brave people</u> share my dreams of space travel.
4. I <u>close my eyes and wish for my own spaceship</u>.
5. <u>The rocket</u> takes me directly to the moon.
6. I <u>am safe and warm in my silver suit</u>.

Read each sentence. Write the letter of the word
that is the noun in the subject.

7. Dreams can seem very real to us.

    A us   **C** Dreams
    B seem   **D** real

8. A nightmare is a really scary dream.

    A nightmare   **C** is
    B dream   **D** scary

9. Some people dream in color.

    A Some   **C** color
    B people   **D** dream

10. Wonderful events can happen in dreams.

    A Wonderful   **C** happen
    B can   **D** events

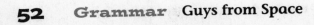

Choosing the Right Nouns

Replace general nouns such as *places* and *things* with nouns that give readers clear word pictures.

- **Not clear:** The green <u>guys</u> left their <u>place</u> in a kind of <u>thing</u>.
- **Clear:** The green <u>aliens</u> left their <u>planet</u> in a <u>flying saucer</u>.

A Replace each underlined noun with an exact noun from the list to make this description stronger. Write the new paragraph.

skyscrapers   planet   whistle   creatures   huts

1. The tiny <u>things</u> jumped onto Earth late one night. **2.** A surprised <u>noise</u> came through their bright blue mouths. **3.** They had never seen such tall <u>buildings</u> before! **4.** Back home they lived in low, round <u>homes</u>. **5.** There was nothing on their faraway <u>place</u> quite like this.

B Add an exact noun of your own to complete each sentence. Write the paragraph.

6. I dreamed about a giant brown _____. **7.** It ran up and licked my _____. **8.** I jumped up onto a _____. **9.** I didn't want that _____ to touch me! **10.** Suddenly, I felt a gentle tap on my _____. **11.** It was my _____, waking me up for school.

C Describe a funny dream you had. Use exact nouns to give your readers a clear picture of what happened.

Singular and Plural Nouns

A **singular noun** names only one person, place, or thing. A **plural noun** names more than one. Most nouns add -**s** to form the plural: **storms.** Add -**es** to a noun that ends in **ch, sh, s, ss,** or **x: couches, ashes, buses, kisses, boxes.** When a noun ends in a consonant and **y,** change the **y** to **i** and then add -**es: bodies.**

Some irregular plural nouns have a special form.

**child/children   foot/feet   goose/geese   man/men
mouse/mice   ox/oxen   person/people   tooth/teeth**

 A Write **S** if the underlined noun is singular.
Write **P** if the noun is plural.

1. A <u>tornado</u> can cause a lot of harm.
2. I watched the <u>storm</u> from my window.
3. Some <u>adults</u> thought the storm was exciting.
4. It blew through our <u>town</u> and out into the fields.

Write the sentences. Underline the singular nouns.
Circle the plural nouns.

5. My brother and his friends were playing outside.
6. In a few seconds, the sky grew dark.
7. The children lay down in a nearby ditch.
8. The wind blew right over their bodies.

B Write the three plural nouns in each sentence.

1. One day, I saw snowflakes, raindrops, and hailstones.
2. People in the streets and fields looked up in surprise.
3. Workers on tall buildings climbed down their ladders.
4. Mothers pushing strollers dashed into open shops.
5. Boys and girls pointed at the clouds.
6. Teachers stopped giving lessons to their classes.
7. The roads and highways filled up with puddles.
8. The parks, lawns, and yards were all soaked.
9. My friends talked about the three storms for days.

C Write the plural form of the noun in ( ).

10. It rained during my birthday (party).
11. The (child) had to run indoors.
12. Mom set up cardboard (box) to sit on.
13. That thunder made our (tooth) chatter.
14. We had cake and (strawberry).
15. We sang songs along with the (radio).
16. May I open all the (gift) now?
17. When the rain stopped, my (guest) ran out to play.
18. We raced through the damp (grass).
19. How soggy are these garden (bench)?
20. Our (foot) were dry at the end of the party.

Review and Assess

Change the underlined singular noun to a plural noun.
Write the new sentences.

1. Many tourists come to the <u>island</u>.
2. People love the quiet <u>beach</u> and warm days.
3. They swim and snorkel with their <u>child</u>.
4. Islanders love welcoming <u>person</u> to their home.
5. Have you heard the <u>story</u> about this island?
6. Wait until you get my <u>postcard</u> from the hotel!
7. Their water <u>glass</u> are in the shape of palm trees.

Write the letter of the plural form of each underlined noun.

8. Horses trot around the <u>trail</u> in the rain forest.

   A trailies   **C** trails
   B trailess   **D** trailes

9. Squirrels perch on the leafy <u>branch</u>.

   A branchies   **C** branchs
   B brancheses   **D** branches

10. Purple flowers hang from the twisted <u>vine</u>.

   A vines   **C** viness
   B vinies   **D** vins

11. People throw <u>penny</u> into the wishing well.

   A pennys   **C** pennyes
   B pennies   **D** pennyies

Using Plural Nouns in Descriptions

Describe plural nouns clearly to create a good word picture. When you spell plural nouns correctly, your readers won't be confused.

- **No:** The <u>mices</u> run past the gray cat.
- **Yes:** The frightened <u>mice</u> run past the gray cat.

A Add a word from the list to make the descriptions lively. Write the plural form of each underlined noun. Then write the new sentences.

leafy	laughing	sandy	cloudy

1. The storm blew over the _____ <u>beach</u>.
2. Rain fell over the _____ <u>child</u> too.
3. I saw the _____ <u>tree</u> shake in the wind.
4. Suddenly, the _____ <u>sky</u> grew lighter.

B Write the correct plural form of each underlined noun. Add your own word to describe the noun. Write the paragraph.

5. The _____ <u>goose</u> began to honk loudly. **6.** Soon, the _____ <u>mouse</u> scampered across the meadow. **7.** A pair of _____ <u>fox</u> raced under the bushes. **8 .** _____ <u>bunny</u> crept into their holes. **9.** As the thunderstorm began, the _____ <u>man</u> stopped working in the field.

C Write a letter that tells about a big storm. Describe singular and plural nouns to make your writing lively and detailed.

Possessive Nouns

A noun that shows ownership is a **possessive noun.** Add an **apostrophe (')** and **-s** to a singular noun to make it possessive.

    iceberg   iceberg**'s** edge

Add an **apostrophe (')** to a plural noun that ends in **-s, -es,** or **-ies** to make it possessive.

    ships   ships**'** flags   berries   berries**'** flavor

Some irregular plural nouns do not end in **-s.** To make these nouns possessive, add an **apostrophe (')** and **-s.**

    women   women**'s** team   people   people**'s** books

 A Write the possessive noun in each sentence.

1. The students' job is to find out about glaciers.
2. Most of Earth's fresh water is stored in glaciers.
3. The snow's layers are packed down.
4. The children's teacher will show a film about ice sheets.
5. Two classmates' reports are about glaciers.

Write the possessive noun in ( ) to complete each sentence.

6. A man from an (explorers, explorers') club will speak to us.
7. All my (friends', friend's) parents are invited to come too.
8. Some of us have seen our (planets, planet's) icy mountains.
9. The (speakers, speaker's) photos were incredible.
10. He told us about walking over one (ridges', ridge's) edge.

B Add an (') or an (') and **-s** to the underlined word in each phrase to form the possessive. Write the phrase. The first one is done for you.

1. the size of the <u>glacier</u> **the glacier's size**
2. the water of the <u>ocean</u>
3. the glaciers of <u>Alaska</u>
4. the subjects of the <u>stories</u>
5. the slides belonging to the <u>school</u>
6. the work of the <u>scientists</u>
7. the color of the <u>ice</u>
8. questions of the <u>people</u>

C Make each noun in the box a possessive noun. Then complete each sentence with one of the possessive nouns. Write the new paragraph.

state	children	glacier
world	uncle	class

9. My uncle has visited all of the _____ continents.
10. He began by exploring his own _____ mountains.
11. His _____ school had a family career day. 12. My _____ adventures excited everyone. 13. Can you believe that he hiked across a _____ surface? 14. My _____ teacher would like him to tell us his adventure stories too.

Review and Assess

Add an apostrophe (') or an (') and -s to the underlined word in each sentence to form the possessive. Write the sentences.

1. I like to flip through my <u>atlas</u> pages.
2. Read these <u>people</u> books about travel.
3. Have you seen the wall maps in both my <u>sisters</u> rooms?
4. I know each <u>continent</u> shape.
5. Some maps show what the <u>Earth</u> surface is like.
6. A globe shows the whole <u>planet</u> shape.

Write the letter of the the correct possessive noun to complete each sentence.

7. The travelers saw some of the _____ wonders.

   A world   **C** worlds's

   B world's   **D** worlds

8. The _____ height amazed the visitors.

   A pyramid's **C** pyramid

   B pyramids   **D** pyramids's

9. One _____ peak looked like a white tower.

   A icebergs   **C** icebergs's

   B icebergs' **D** iceberg's

10. Many birds live in these _____ trees.

   A forest   **C** forests'

   B forests   **D** forests's

Using Possessive Nouns in Descriptions

Possessive nouns can make your writing less wordy. By using fewer words, your sentences will sound smoother.

- The <u>job of the sailor</u> can be exciting.
- The <u>sailor's job</u> can be exciting.

A Replace each underlined group of words with a phrase that has a possessive noun. Write the new paragraph.

1. The <u>captain of the ship</u> steered carefully. **2.** The <u>end of the trip</u> was almost here. **3.** The tired captain saw the <u>smiles of the passengers</u>. **4.** They had loved seeing the <u>bodies of the whales</u> leap from the water. **5.** What big waves the <u>splashes of the flukes</u> made! **6.** The <u>dock of the boat</u> was in plain sight. **7.** Passengers shook the <u>hand of the captain</u> as they left.

B Add your own possessive noun to each sentence. Write the sentences.

8. My _____ house is by a lake.
9. The _____ water is icy cold.
10. After a swim, the _____ rays feel warm.
11. We spot a _____ bright wings.
12. The _____ sweet smell fills the air.
13. My _____ picnic lunch tastes yummy.

C Write a description about a trip you took. Use possessive nouns to make your sentences less wordy.

Common and Proper Nouns

Common nouns name any person, place, or thing. **Proper nouns** name a particular person, place, or thing. They begin with a capital letter. Capitalize each important word in a proper noun.

Common nouns: We will go to the <u>city</u> one <u>day</u>.
Proper nouns: We will go to <u>Houston</u> on <u>Tuesday</u>.

A Write **C** if the underlined noun in the sentence is a common noun. Write **P** if the noun is a proper noun.

   1. The young <u>birds</u> cannot fly.
   2. A little girl named <u>Halla</u> guards them carefully.
   3. The other children of <u>Heimaey Island</u> help too.
   4. Soon the birds will fly away from the high <u>cliffs</u>.
   5. They never go far from the <u>Arctic Circle</u>.

Write the sentences. Underline each common noun and circle each proper noun.

   6. The Everglades is a giant wetland.
   7. It covers acres of land in southern Florida.
   8. Are there marshes all over the United States?
   9. In November, the colorful spoonbills start to breed.
  10. Huge alligators live in wetlands in Louisiana.
  11. Texas and other states are protecting these areas.

B Write all the common nouns in one column. Write all the proper nouns in another column. Capitalize the proper nouns.

1. river   amazon river
2. california   state
3. town   westport
4. author   richard peck
5. july   month
6. girl   tara
7. flag day   holiday
8. dentist   dr. green
9. mr. chiang   principal
10. country   iceland
11. mt. rainier   hills

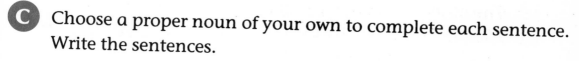

C Choose a proper noun of your own to complete each sentence. Write the sentences.

12. I live in the state of _____.
13. We have a park called _____.
14. A river in our state is the _____.
15. My state's capital is _____.
16. We saw some beautiful birds at the _____.
17. Our class went on a trip to the _____.

Review and Assess

Write the sentences with proper nouns capitalized correctly.
Underline each common noun. Circle each proper noun.

1. I saw a special movie about africa.
2. A veterinarian went to help animals in kenya.
3. She took an airplane to the busy city of nairobi.
4. Then she went by bus to tsavo national park.
5. She also visited mount kenya, which is a volcano.

Read each group of words. Write the letter of the words or word
that is a proper noun.

6. **A** Midway Airport   **C** bridge
   B airport   **D** highway

7. **A** year   **C** May
   B week   **D** month

8. **A** city   **C** country
   B Sweden   **D** town

9. **A** skyscraper   **C** Empire State Building
   B factory   **D** house

10. **A** runway   **C** airplane
    B flight   **D** Corus Airlines

Using Proper Nouns in Descriptions

Read the sentences below. See how proper nouns can make a sentence clearer.

- She sniffed the flowers in the garden.
- Elena sniffed the flowers in Westbury Gardens.

A Replace each underlined word or words with a proper noun from the list.

> Big Buddy   Mrs. Strauss   Halsey Nature Park
> Interstate 22   Africa

   1. Our class went on a tour of <u>the park</u>. **2.** We took the bus on <u>a road</u>. **3.** <u>A lady</u>, the park ranger, explained everything to us. **4.** What a bumpy ride I took on <u>an animal</u>! **5.** He is an elephant from <u>another continent</u>.

B Complete each sentence with a proper noun of your own. Use the clues in ( ).

   6. _____ has leafy trees. (street)
   7. The trees in _____ give us cool shade. (park)
   8. _____ and _____ ring their bicycle bells as they ride. (names)
   9. A breeze ruffles the thick grass near _____. (river)

C Write a short description of a park or zoo you have visited. Use two proper nouns.

Writing a Description

A **test** may ask you to write a description. Use images and sense words to make your descriptive writing come alive. Follow the tips below.

ORDER

Group your details in a clear order, such as from top to bottom.

Understand the prompt. Know what you have to do. Read the prompt carefully. A prompt for a description could look like this:

> **Write a descriptive paragraph about a place that is special to you. Help people use their senses to picture your place.**

Key words and phrases are *descriptive, place that is special,* and *senses.*

Find a good topic. Choose a place you know well. It might be a vacation spot or a place in your neighborhood.

Organize your ideas. For this assignment, you could make a description web on scratch paper. Write your topic in the center circle. Write details about that place in connected circles.

tall reeds
thick grasses

screeching birds
croaking bullfrogs

Sheffield Marsh

Write a good beginning. Your opening sentence sets the scene. A clear topic sentence helps readers get the picture.

Develop and elaborate ideas. Use the information in your web. Include sense words that give your readers a vivid picture.

Write a strong ending. Save a strong detail for the end.

Check your work. Read your description and look for anything you would like to fix or change.

See how this description answers the prompt, has a strong opening and closing, and uses vivid details and sense words.

1 — Marshes are alive with animals, birds, and plants.
2 — Sheffield Marsh is one of my favorite places. It is only a few miles from my house, but it feels very far away.
3 — Screeching birds fly through the sky. Deer and rabbits graze at the edge of the marsh. Silver fish swim through the water, and bullfrogs croak in the tall reeds.

What a sweet smell the marsh plants have! You can also smell the tiny wildflowers that grow there. The water might seem muddy, but my dad says marshes clean — 4 themselves. That is why so many animals can live there.
5 — The marsh is a whole world. I hope it never changes.

1. The opening sentence sets the scene.
2. A proper noun makes the location clear.
3. Vivid words help readers use their senses.
4. The description builds up to important information.
5. The ending has a strong message for the reader.

Writing a Description for Tests **67**

Verbs

Action verbs are words that show what someone or something does. **Linking verbs** do not show action. They link, or join, a subject to a word in the predicate. *Am, is, are, was,* and *were* are forms of the linking verb *be.*

Action verb: Rain <u>hits</u> the sidewalks.
Linking verb: The roads <u>were</u> full of water.

A One of the underlined words in each sentence is a verb. Write that word.

   1. Mrs. Stewart <u>reads</u> a story to the <u>class.</u>
   2. It <u>is</u> a tale about a <u>magic</u> pebble.
   3. The pebble <u>gives</u> people three <u>wishes.</u>
   4. We <u>listen</u> closely to <u>the</u> story.
   5. It <u>ends</u> <u>happily</u> for all.

Write the sentences. Underline the verb in each sentence.

   6. I wrote a poem last night.
   7. My poem is about the deep winter snow.
   8. It describes the trees and the white fields.
   9. I read it to my class this morning.
  10. Some students liked it very much.
  11. They actually clapped for me!
  12. I tacked my poem to the bulletin board.

B Write the verbs. Write **A** after each action verb. Write **L** after each linking verb.

1. Writers often type their stories on computers.
2. They choose their ideas carefully.
3. A good plot is important to a story.
4. Interesting characters are important too.
5. Some writers draw their own pictures.
6. I borrowed some picture books.
7. These were always my favorites.
8. I found a book under my bed!

C Add a verb of your own to complete each sentence. Write the sentences. Then write **A** if you used an action verb and **L** if you used a linking verb.

9. The children _____ a snowman today.
10. Chris _____ a carrot nose on the snowman.
11. Pat _____ a scarf around its neck.
12. The wind _____ through the trees.
13. Winter _____ my favorite season.

Review and Assess

Write the sentences. Underline each verb. Write **A** if the verb is an action verb. Write **L** if the verb is a linking verb.

1. My mother writes books for children.
2. I save all of her books.
3. Mom is one of my favorite authors.
4. My friends were happy with her books.
5. She read one of her stories aloud.
6. Afterward, the children thanked her.

Read each sentence. Write the letter of the word that is a verb.

7. I opened my box of paints.

     A my   **C** paints

     B of   **D** opened

8. Then I dipped my paintbrush into the water jar.

     A dipped   **C** water

     B paintbrush **D** jar

9. All the colors are fresh and bright.

     A colors   **C** are

     B fresh   **D** All

10. I painted an exciting picture.

      A an   **C** picture

      B painted   **D** I

Using Vivid Verbs in Your Writing

Strong verbs make your writing come alive. See how vivid verbs make the new sentences more exciting.

- Our cat <u>walks</u> around my room. He <u>is</u> on my lap.
- Our cat <u>slinks</u> around my room. He <u>purrs</u> on my lap.

A Replace each underlined verb with a verb from the list. Write the new paragraph.

     pop   grab   cheer   play   zoom   stare

1. When I <u>get</u> a book off the shelf, I am ready to use my imagination. **2.** Exciting ideas <u>come</u> into my head. **3.** But when I <u>am</u> in a game outdoors, I use my whole body. **4.** My feet <u>go</u> along the playground like rockets. **5.** My friends <u>look</u> at me. **6.** They <u>speak</u> when I race by!

B Write four sentences that compare and contrast what you do at home and what you do at school. Choose verbs from the list below or use verbs of your own.

    Home: read, wash, nap, cook, dig, dream
    School: write, read, paint, race, laugh, sing

C Write a short letter to a friend that compares and contrasts two kinds of work that you do around your home. Use vivid verbs to make your letter come alive.

Verbs in Sentences

A verb is the main word in the predicate, the part of a sentence that tells what the subject is or does. You can combine the predicates of sentences that have the same subject with the words *and* or *or*.

> The bear <u>growled.</u> The bear <u>roared.</u>
> The bear <u>growled and roared.</u>

A verb can be two words. The **main verb** is the most important word. The **helping verb** comes before it. *Am, is, are, was, were, has, had,* and *have* are often used as helping verbs.

> The bear <u>has</u> <u>licked</u> the honey.   I <u>am</u> <u>taking</u> a trip.

 A The complete predicate is underlined in each sentence. Write the verb.

1. Lazy Bear <u>sleeps all day long.</u>
2. Mr. and Mrs. Hare <u>worry about their children.</u>
3. The Hares <u>hatch a clever plan.</u>
4. They <u>play a trick on poor old Bear.</u>
5. They <u>gather the crops for themselves.</u>

Write the sentences. Underline the complete predicate. Write the verb.

6. David and Marie planted a vegetable garden.
7. Their family worked very hard.
8. They picked a crop of carrots.

B A verb is underlined in each sentence. Write **M** if it is a main verb. Write **H** if it is a helping verb.

1. Anna had <u>worked</u> in the garden yesterday.
2. Her sister <u>had</u> helped too.
3. They had <u>taken</u> the tools from the shed.
4. "You <u>have</u> forgotten to get the shovel," said Anna's sister.
5. "I had <u>put</u> the shovel next to the tree," Anna answered.
6. Anna is <u>digging</u> several holes in the ground.
7. Both children <u>are</u> placing a seed in each hole.
8. The tired girls are <u>finishing</u> their job very late.

C Combine the predicates in each pair of sentences. Write the new sentences.

9. Hollyhoke Farm grows many kinds of berries.
   Hollyhoke Farm sells many kinds of berries.

10. The farmer waters all of the berries.
    The farmer fertilizes all of the berries.

11. A smiling woman picks a bunch of blueberries.
    A smiling woman washes a bunch of blueberries.

12. My friend and I taste the blueberries.
    My friend and I buy the blueberries.

13. That night, we bake two delicious blueberry pies.
    That night, we eat two delicious blueberry pies.

Review and Assess

The predicate in each sentence is underlined. Write the verb or verbs in each sentence.

1. Orchids <u>bloom in my aunt's greenhouse.</u>
2. She <u>has grown these lovely flowers for many years.</u>
3. One orchid plant <u>clings to a bush.</u>
4. My aunt <u>sprays this special plant with water.</u>
5. It <u>grows and thrives without soil.</u>
6. My aunt <u>had won first prize for her orchids at the fair.</u>

Read each sentence. Write the letter that shows the verb in each sentence.

7. Aunt Sally has grown three types of orchids in pots.

   A has   **C** grown three

   B grown   **D** has grown

8. One plant has produced tiny orange blossoms.

   A has   **C** has produced

   B produced   **D** produced tiny

9. Aunt Sally has taught me a lot about flowers.

   A has taught   **C** has taught me

   B taught   **D** taught me

10. I am raising some orchids too.

    A am   **C** raising

    B am raising   **D** raising some

Replacing *Get, Put,* and *Take*

Try not to use verbs such as *get, put,* and *take* too often. Replace these words with strong verbs that make your ideas clear.

- I <u>get</u> a shopping cart. Then I <u>take</u> some fruit.
  The cashier <u>puts</u> it in a bag. **(dull verbs)**
- I <u>grab</u> a shopping cart. Then I <u>weigh</u> some fruit.
  The cashier <u>packs</u> it in a bag. **(strong verbs)**

A Write a verb from the list to replace each underlined verb.

      steal   shoves   throws

1. Paul <u>puts</u> his peas under the plate.
2. The baby <u>gets</u> his carrots on the floor.
3. The two cats <u>take</u> some of the beef from the plate.

B Complete the sentences by adding strong verbs of your own. Then add a closing sentence.

    4. My brother and I want to _____ a special meal. 5. This morning, we _____ for some fresh vegetables. 6. I _____ the green beans and broccoli on the scale. 7. We always _____ apples and peaches for dessert. 8. On the way home, I _____ on the sidewalk. 9. Fruit _____ out of the bag. 10. _____

C Write a paragraph that compares a food you like with a food you don't like. Replace dull verbs with strong, interesting verbs.

Verb Tenses

A verb in the **present tense** shows action happening now. Many present-tense verbs end with **-s** or **-es**: She <u>walks</u>. Verbs that end in a **consonant** and **y** change the **y** to **i** before adding **-es**: He <u>cries</u>.

A verb in the **past tense** shows action that has already happened. Add **-ed** to many past-tense verbs: He <u>walked</u>. Some verbs are spelled differently in the past tense.

- For most one-syllable verbs that end in a single vowel and a consonant, double the final consonant and add **–ed**: She <u>clapped</u> her hands.
- When a verb ends in a **consonant** and **y,** change the **y** to **i** before adding **-ed**: We <u>hurried</u> home.

A verb in the **future tense** shows action that will happen. Verbs in the future tense use the helping verb **will**: I <u>will</u> go.

Verb	Present Tense	Past Tense	Future Tense
walk	The dog walks.	Dad walked.	Mom will walk.
cry	Nina cries.	We cried.	He will cry.
skip	We skip.	I skipped.	Dave will skip.

 Write the word or words that are the verb in each sentence.

1. Mr. McDonald trains guide dogs.
2. He picked our puppy for us.
3. Sparky will do a good job.
4. Dad thanked Mr. McDonald for the help.

B Write the verb in ( ) that correctly completes each sentence.

1. Last night my dog (barks, barked) at the TV.
2. He (learns, learned) to sit when we brought him home.
3. I (prepare, prepared) him a treat that day.
4. Now he (begs, begged) almost every time he sits!
5. Tomorrow we (worked, will work) on another trick.
6. I (praise, praised) him for his good work yesterday.
7. Our cat (watched, will watch) while I taught the dog.
8. Next time, we all (played, will play) together.
9. Last night, my sister (cry, cried) for a treat too.

C Change each underlined verb to the tense in ( ).

10. Some dogs <u>enjoyed</u> search and rescue work. (present)
11. They <u>find</u> lost people anywhere. (future)
12. Rescue dogs <u>carry</u> many people to safety. (past)
13. They <u>will search</u> in dangerous places. (past)
14. These dogs <u>behaved</u> very bravely. (present)
15. I <u>copy</u> a report about these animals. (past)
16. My dad <u>believed</u> they are real heroes. (present)
17. My friends and I <u>will agree</u> with him. (present)

Review and Assess

Write the verb in ( ) that correctly completes each sentence.

1. I (see, will see) a dog show tomorrow.
2. Last year, I (attend, attended) a cat show.
3. Do you (enjoy, will enjoy) animal competitions?
4. Some dogs already (competed, will compete) for prizes.
5. Tomorrow judges (named, will name) winners.
6. We (will travel, traveled) to tomorrow's show by car.

Write the letter of the verb that completes each sentence.
Use the tense in ( ).

7. Working dogs _____ sheep and cows on the ranch. (present)

   A herds   **C** herded
   B herd   **D** will herd

8. Some dogs _____ people from danger. (past)

   A drags   **C** dragged
   B dragging **D** draged

9. I _____ the sporting dogs compete. (present)

   A watch   **C** watched
   B will watch **D** watches

10. Maybe the spaniel _____ the blue ribbon. (future)

    A wins   **C** won
    B win   **D** will win

Using Correct Verb Tenses in Your Writing

Sometimes a writer compares how things were in the past with how they are now. Interesting verbs and correct tenses tell the story.

- I <u>gobbled</u> raisins when I was little. Now I <u>chew</u> raw carrots.

A Choose an interesting verb from the list to replace each underlined verb. Change each verb to the correct tense.

    mold   clutch   scribble   paint   guide

1. My little sister <u>held</u> a doll all the time when she was a baby. **2.** Now she <u>writes</u> with her new crayons. **3.** Last week, we <u>made</u> a picture together. **4.** When she is older, she will <u>make</u> something out of clay. **5.** I will <u>hold</u> her hands as she works.

B Complete each sentence with a strong verb of your own. Write the new sentences. Make sure you use the correct verb tense.

  6. Last year, my parents _____ Bowser to sit and beg.
  7. These days, they _____ Bowser's polite habits.
  8. When we smile at him, he _____ up and licks our faces.
  9. He _____ at my hand when it's time to go for a walk.

C Write an e-mail to a friend that tells about a game you liked when you were little and a game you enjoy now. Use verb tenses that show your friend how things have changed.

Forms of Regular Verbs

In your writing, you use different forms of a verb for different tenses. The verbs below have similar forms. They are called **regular verbs.** See how each verb works, or agrees, with its subject.

-s form	*-ing* form	*-ed* form
Jim <u>works</u>.	He <u>is working</u>.	He <u>worked</u>.
He <u>cooks</u>.	We <u>are cooking</u>.	They <u>cooked</u>.

A Choose the form of the verb that makes sense in each sentence. Write the sentences.

1. Mom (designing, designs) quilts to sell.
2. She (finished, finishes) five quilts last year.
3. She (patch, patched) together some pieces.
4. Mom is (sewed, sewing) the pieces now.
5. I (helped, help) her with the easy parts yesterday.

Write each sentence, using the correct form of the verb.

6. Now Mom is (spell) my name with red letters.
7. I was (hope) that the quilt was for me.
8. It (look) beautiful now that it is done.
9. Mom is (start) another quilt.
10. It (show) a lion cub.
11. My little brother (like) lions now.
12. He is (make) his own square.

B Write the sentences using the correct form of the underlined verb.

1. Leong <u>spelling</u> difficult words before.
2. Now he will <u>spelled</u> another word.
3. Visitors <u>watch</u> him carefully now.
4. Leong <u>listen</u> to the new word as the teacher reads it.
5. Leong <u>look</u> straight ahead as he speaks.
6. After he finished, Leong <u>walk</u> to his seat.
7. Then everyone was <u>cheered</u> for him!
8. Soon, Mom and Dad will <u>praised</u> his work.
9. His brother is <u>jumps</u> for joy now.
10. After the contest, his teacher <u>place</u> a ribbon around his neck.

C Match the sentence on the left with the correct verb form on the right. Write the complete sentence.

11. I am _____ a songwriting contest.
12. Everyone _____ a song.
13. Ms. Harmon _____ these contests.
14. I am _____ on my song.
15. It _____ good to me.
16. The tune _____ me.

   a. judges
   b. pleases
   c. creates
   d. sounds
   e. working
   f. entering

Review and Assess

Choose the correct form of the verb to complete each sentence.
Write the sentences.

1. Do you (like, liking) nicknames?
2. Karen always (laugh, laughs) about her special name.
3. Her family (calls, calling) her "Bunny."
4. Bunnies (hop, hops) around Karen's yard.
5. Karen sometimes (acts, acting) very lively too.
6. Sometimes, nicknames (show, showing) how people act.

Write the letter of the verb form that completes
each sentence.

7. The little mouse _____ bravely.

   A acted   **C** were acting

   B are acted   **D** are acting

8. It _____ up to the table for a snack.

   A have scampered   **C** were scampering

   B scampered   **D** are scampering

9. A cat _____ around the room.

   A were prowling   **C** was prowling

   B is prowled   **D** were prowled

10. The mouse _____ up for a piece of cheese anyway.

    A jumped   **C** was jumped

    B jumping   **D** were jumping

Changing Verb Tenses

Choose verb tenses carefully to make ideas clear. Think about when the action is happening before you change tenses.

- Last night, the animal shelter <u>called</u> my mom. Today, she <u>is visiting</u> the shelter to look at a new kitten. Tonight, our new kitten <u>will share</u> my blanket.

A Make the writing clear by changing any underlined verb that is in the wrong tense. Write the new paragraph.

   1. Yesterday, I <u>raced</u> to my friend's house. **2.** I <u>want</u> to play with Dawn's new dog. **3.** Dawn <u>name</u> the dog Chocolate because of his brown fur. **4.** The dog <u>bound</u> around the house at first. **5.** Now he <u>dozes</u> on her lap every afternoon.

B Write two sentences that compare and contrast what you did when you were a baby and what you do now. You might describe your favorite food, games, or music at both ages.

C Write a letter to a friend that compares and contrasts what you did on Saturday and Sunday. Use verb forms that clearly show when the action happened.

Forms of Irregular Verbs

Verbs that do not add **-ed** to show past action are called **irregular verbs.** Because irregular verbs do not follow a regular pattern, you must remember their spellings. Here are some irregular verbs.

Present	Past	Past with *has, have,* or *had*
begin	began	*(has, have, had)* begun
do	did	*(has, have, had)* done
find	found	*(has, have, had)* found
give	gave	*(has, have, had)* given
go	went	*(has, have, had)* gone
run	ran	*(has, have, had)* run
see	saw	*(has, have, had)* seen
take	took	*(has, have, had)* taken
think	thought	*(has, have, had)* thought
wear	wore	*(has, have, had)* worn

 A Choose the correct form of the irregular verb in ( ) to complete each sentence. Write the verb.

1. My grandfather (took, taken) many photographs.
2. I have (saw, seen) pictures of Mom as a child.
3. She (go, went) to dance class, just as I did.
4. I once (think, thought) she hated dancing.
5. Then I (find, found) an old photo of her.
6. She (wore, worn) a tutu and tights!

B Write each sentence with the past form of the underlined verb. Each answer will be one word.

1. I <u>run</u> around the path in the park.
2. Each workout <u>begins</u> at 3:30 in the afternoon.
3. I <u>do</u> a quick stretch before the run.
4. Afterward, I <u>take</u> a cool shower.
5. I <u>go</u> to track team practice every day.
6. I <u>see</u> one marathon.
7. My mother <u>give</u> water to the runners.
8. Every runner <u>wear</u> a starting number.
9. I <u>write</u> about the race in my journal.

C Write each sentence with the past form of the verb in ( ) that makes sense.

10. I have (begin) to keep a journal.
11. I have (give) my journal a name.
12. I (take) the name from a movie.
13. Have you (saw) *My Secret Life?*
14. It is about a girl who has (go) to Mars.
15. There she (find) a dog named Ink.
16. She (do) everything she could for Ink.
17. Unfortunately, he (run) away.
18. I still (think) Ink was a good name for a journal.

Review and Assess

Choose the correct form of the verb in ( ) to complete each sentence. Write the sentence.

1. Who (run, ran) in yesterday's race?
2. All the runners (wear, wore) red T-shirts.
3. We (took, take) pictures.
4. I (seen, saw) the whole thing from the bleachers.
5. A slow runner suddenly (began, begun) to catch up.
6. Before I knew it, she had (took, taken) the lead.

Write the letter of the verb that makes sense in each sentence.

7. Alex _____ a new bicycle last week.

    A got   **C** gotted
    B is got   **D** will get

8. He _____ to outgrow the old bike.

    A begun   **C** were beginning
    B had begun   **D** begin

9. He _____ the new bike was beautiful.

    A think   **C** thought
    B thoughted   **D** thinked

10. Alex _____ pictures of his bike.

    A has took   **C** take
    B has taken   **D** taked

Choosing Correct Forms of Verbs

Always use the correct form of verbs in your writing.

- My little brother and I are so much alike. He <u>giggles</u> just like I do. We both <u>wrinkle</u> our noses. He <u>has grown</u> as tall as I am.

A Complete the following paragraph by writing the correct form of the verb in ( ). Refer to the chart on page 84.

1. Yesterday Kara and Joe (find) some pretty colored paper. **2.** They (think) about what they could make with it. **3.** Kara remembered that she had (see) a TV show about paper folding. **4.** Today they have (begin) to create their projects. **5.** When he is finished, Joe will (give) his artwork to his mom.

B Use verbs from the chart on page 84 to complete the paragraph. Choose the correct form of each verb. Then finish the last sentence.

6. Each day, Carmen wakes up and _____ her favorite jeans. **7.** She has _____ them more times than any others. **8.** She _____ that they are her lucky jeans. **9.** When she wears them, she _____ faster and jumps higher than her friends. **10.** Of all Carmen's clothes, _____.

C Write a paragraph that compares and contrasts your two favorite activities. Use correct verb tense to show the action.

Writing a Comparison/ Contrast Paragraph

A **test** may ask you to write a comparison/contrast paragraph. Use words that show likenesses *(and, also, both)* and differences *(although, but)*. Follow the tips below.

Understand the prompt. Read the prompt carefully. A prompt for a comparison/contrast paragraph could look like this:

> **Write a paragraph comparing and contrasting two characters from stories your class has read. Show how they are alike and different.**

Key phrases are *comparing and contrasting, stories your class has read,* and *alike and different.*

GROUP DETAILS

Tell about likenesses first, and then describe differences.

Find a good topic. Choose stories with characters you can compare and contrast.

Organize your ideas. Make a comparison/contrast organizer on scratch paper like the one below. Write details about the characters in the *Same* and *Different* sections.

Topic Sentence Hare and Ananse are alike and different.			
SAME		**DIFFERENT**	
Character: Hare	**Character:** Ananse	**Character:** Hare	**Character:** Ananse
Plays a trick	Plays a trick	Cares for family	Cares for himself
Keeps food	Keeps food	Has last laugh	Is fooled

Write a good beginning. Draw your reader in.

Develop and elaborate ideas. Build on your organizer.

Write a strong ending. Sum up your ideas in the last sentence.

Check your work. This is the time to change what you want.

See how the paragraph below follows the prompt, has a good topic sentence and conclusion, and uses transition words.

Two Tricksters

1 — Hare and Ananse are alike and different. Each character played a trick on a friend. First, Hare offered Bear the tops of his crops, then the bottoms. Next, he offered the tops and bottoms. Each time, he kept the best parts. Ananse also offered a friend a feast but didn't let him eat. He told Akye to wash his dirty hands first. While Akye was washing, Ananse ate the food.

4 — Hare and Ananse are also different. Hare plays the trick because his children need food, but Ananse is selfish.

5 — At the end, Hare has the last laugh, but Ananse is fooled.

1. The topic sentence introduces the subject clearly.
2. Order words make the paragraphs easy to follow.
3. Verb forms are correct.
4. The comparison and contrast points are clear.
5. The conclusion wraps up the details.

Adjectives

· ·

An **adjective** is a word that describes a noun. Adjectives can tell how a person, place, or thing looks, tastes, sounds, feels, or smells. Adjectives can also tell how much or how many.

The adjectives *a, an,* and *the* are called **articles**. Articles go before nouns and sometimes before other adjectives. Use *a* before singular nouns that begin with a consonant. Use *an* before singular nouns that begin with a vowel. Use *the* before singular nouns or plural nouns.

· ·

- Tricky Coyote had <u>a</u> plan. <u>Some</u> water was in <u>an</u> <u>empty</u> well.
- Coyote climbed over <u>two</u> <u>white</u> goats.

A Write the adjective that describes each underlined noun.

1. Fox's guest was hungry <u>Stork</u>.
2. "What delicious <u>smell</u> is that?"
3. Fox pointed to two <u>bowls</u> of soup.
4. Stork's beak would not fit into the <u>bowls</u>.

Write the sentences. Underline the articles. Circle other adjectives in the sentences.

5. Stork invited the fox for a tasty meal.
6. Stork put the meal in a narrow jar.
7. The jar worked with Stork's thin beak.

B A noun is underlined in each sentence. Write the adjective or adjectives that tell more about the underlined noun.

1. A hungry <u>wolf</u> met a dog on the road.
2. The dog told him where to get healthful <u>food</u>.
3. A kind <u>master</u> could feed the wolf.
4. Wolf asked the tame <u>animal</u> why he wore a collar.
5. The gentle <u>dog</u> was chained up at night.
6. Wild <u>Wolf</u> did not want that to happen to him!

C Add an adjective from the box or one of your own to each sentence. Write the new sentences.

some	huge	hungry	orange	frosty	crunchy

7. In winter, I make a _____ feast for wild animals.
8. Many _____ creatures come to our yard. 9. I leave out _____ nuts for the squirrels. 10. I pour a bag of _____ bird seed into the feeder. 11. Rabbits and deer like the _____ carrots I leave by the fence. 12. I peek through the _____ window to watch the visitors eat.

Review and Assess

Write the sentences. Circle each article. Underline the other adjectives.

1. I found some simple recipes in a magazine.
2. One recipe shows how to make a wonderful pie.
3. My big sister will help me make the crust.
4. The recipe says to cut thin strips of dough.
5. The golden crust will have a pretty pattern.

Write the letter of the adjective that best completes each sentence.

6. _____ people enjoy cooking favorite foods.

   A Angry   C Many
   B Red   D No

7. My aunt prepares _____ tortillas for dinner.

   A crisp   C noisy
   B one   D busy

8. My dad cooks a _____ pudding called flan.

   A few   C loud
   B sweet   D long

9. My brother can make a bowl of _____ popcorn.

   A old   C thin
   B lucky   D tasty

Using Clear Adjectives in a How-to Report

In how-to writing, use adjectives to show exactly how something looks, sounds, feels, tastes, or smells.

- Stir the <u>creamy</u> mixture until it is <u>light</u> and <u>yellow</u>.

A Make the following instructions clear by adding the adjectives below or adjectives of your own. Write the new paragraph.

> delicious   sweet   heated   two   first

> **1.** You can make _____ French toast. **2.** The _____ step is to beat together an egg and milk. **3.** Next, dip _____ slices of bread in the mixture. **4.** Place the bread in a _____ pan and fry both sides. **5.** Add _____ toppings and enjoy.

B Add adjectives of your own to make these steps clear. Then write an ending sentence to sum up the instructions.

> **6.** Washing your bike is not a _____ job. **7.** First, find some _____ rags. **8.** Then get a _____ pail. **9.** Fill it with _____ water and liquid soap. **10.** After soaping your bike, rinse it with a _____ hose and dry it. **11.** Now admire your _____ bike.

C Write instructions for something you know how to make. Remember to tell how things should look, sound, or smell.

Comparative and Superlative Adjectives

Some adjectives make comparisons. To compare two people, places, or things, you usually add **-er** to the adjective. These are called **comparative adjectives**. To compare three or more things, you usually add **-est** to the adjective. These are called **superlative adjectives**.

My sister is **younger** than I am.
The baby is the **youngest** of all.

A Write the sentences. Underline the adjectives that compare.

1. The den is the warmest room, so I play my drums there.
2. My dog Buttercup's bark is louder than my drums!
3. He is our oldest dog.
4. The house was quieter before he arrived.

Write **C** if the underlined adjective is a comparative adjective. Write **S** if it is a superlative adjective.

5. My grandmother is our <u>oldest</u> family member.
6. Her kitchen is the <u>brightest</u> room in her house.
7. She roasts the <u>freshest</u> chickens she can find.
8. Grandma cooks in the <u>largest</u> pot of all.
9. In her kitchen, she moves <u>faster</u> than lightning.

B Complete each sentence with the correct form of the adjective in ( ). Write the sentences.

1. Chinese New Year is the (louder, loudest) day of all.
2. Yesterday was (calmer, calmest) than today.
3. Sam felt like the (richest, richer) boy in town.
4. He got a (largest, larger) gift this year than last year.
5. But even the (smaller, smallest) toys cost too much.

C Write the correct form of the adjective in ( ) to complete each sentence.

6. This banner is _____ than my arm! (long)
7. Ani is wearing _____ socks than Lu. (bright)
8. Ani's shirt is _____ than the sky. (blue)
9. That dragon is the _____ one of all! (large)
10. The colorful lion is _____ than the dragon. (fast)
11. This balloon is _____ than that one. (round)
12. Wow, the lion is _____ than that building. (tall)
13. Last year's floats were _____ than this year's floats. (small)

Grammar Sam and the Lucky Money **95**

Review and Assess

Write the correct form of the adjective in ( ) to complete each sentence.

1. The afternoon was _____ than the morning. (cold)
2. The snowdrifts were _____ than the cars. (high)
3. Sheila was the _____ of all the children in our car. (loud)

Write the letter of the word that is an adjective that compares.

4. Little Al blew up the longest balloon of all.

   A Al   **C** birthday
   B longest   **D** party

5. The boy ate a smaller piece of cake than his dad did.

   A smaller   **C** piece
   B cake   **D** dad

6. Excited Al was happier after he ate his cake.

   A Excited   **C** happier
   B ate   **D** after

7. He was the youngest child at the noisy party.

   A He   **C** party
   B noisy   **D** youngest

Using Adjectives to Make Comparisons

Writers have many tools to make their instructions clear. Comparative and superlative adjectives tell exactly what to do.

- This handy book explains how to build a <u>stronger</u> treehouse, make the <u>largest</u> snowman, or design the <u>fiercest</u> mask.

A Write an opening sentence for this how-to paragraph. Change the underlined adjectives to adjectives that compare.

1. _____ **2.** Roll the <u>large</u> of the three snowballs for the bottom. **3.** For the snowman's middle, make a slightly <u>small</u> ball. **4.** The <u>small</u> ball of all will be the head. **5.** You can use pebbles for eyes, but I use charcoal because it is <u>dark</u>. **6.** Use a carrot that is <u>long</u> than your finger for the nose.

B Add adjectives that compare to improve the sentences. Then add a closing sentence. Write the paragraph.

7. On the Fourth of July, we watch the _____ fireworks in the area. **8.** Try to get the _____ seats to the display. **9.** Bring the _____ blankets you can find to sit on the grass. **10.** Last year, the fireworks were on the _____ day of the year. **11.** _____

C Write a paragraph telling how to get ready for a holiday celebration. Use at least one adjective that compares.

Adverbs

An **adverb** is a word that can describe a verb. An adverb tells *when*, *where*, or *how* an action happens. Most adverbs that tell *how* end in **-ly.**

> **How:** Sugar cookies bake <u>quickly</u>. **When:** We made some <u>today</u>. **Where:** Put the cookies <u>there</u>.

Adverbs can also be used to compare actions. To compare two actions, add **-er** to many adverbs. To compare three or more actions, add **-est.** For most adverbs that end in **-ly,** use *more* or *most* instead of **-er** or **-est.**

> Cookies bake <u>faster</u> than cakes.
> The butter cookies bake <u>more quickly</u> than the oatmeal cookies.

Some adverbs that tell about time are *often, soon, today,* and *now.* Other common adverbs are *together, almost, here,* and *there.*

 A In each sentence, a verb is underlined. Write the adverb.

1. I <u>followed</u> the cookie recipe exactly.
2. This recipe <u>comes</u> directly from Sweden.
3. Swedish bakers often <u>put</u> sweet jam on these treats.
4. Everyone in my family <u>eats</u> the cookies more slowly than I.
5. Soon we <u>will bake</u> some Greek pastries.
6. Carefully we <u>chop</u> nuts for the filling.
7. <u>Roll</u> the dough gently so it doesn't crumble.

B Write each sentence with the correct form of the adverb in ( ).

1. My brother shouts (louder, loudest) than thunder.
2. Lightning travels (faster, fastest) than the speediest runner.
3. I closed my window (more quickly, quickly) than Mom did.
4. One clap of thunder rings out (louder, loudest) of all.
5. We ran to the basement (rapidly, more rapidly) than Dad.
6. The wind roars (more fiercely, most fiercely) than a lion.
7. Birds nestle (deeper, deepest) in the trees than before.
8. The lightning flashes (brighter, brightest) than the sun.
9. Leaves fly (more swiftly, most swiftly) than birds.

C Change the adverb in ( ) to its correct form. Write the sentences.

10. Grandpa and I talk (softer).
11. I speak (quickly) than my grandpa does.
12. Today, he woke me (urgently) than usual.
13. He waited (patiently) than I could have.
14. We were going on a trip (soon) than we planned.
15. Luckily, I eat (fast) than a goat!

Review and Assess

Write each sentence. Underline the verb. Circle the adverb.

1. Yesterday, I visited my aunt.
2. I gladly helped her with the cooking.
3. She carefully showed me how to make pancakes.
4. Then we ate all of them!
5. I am planning another visit already.

Write the letter of the word or words that make sense in each sentence.

6. The wind blew _____ than a freight train's whistle.

   A loudly   **C** louder
   B loud   **D** most loudly

7. The clouds gathered _____ in the sky.

   A darkly   **C** dark
   B most dark   **D** more dark

8. My boots slipped _____ into the giant puddles.

   A more deepest **C** deeply
   B most deep   **D** most deepest

9. _____ I was completely soaked.

   A Together   **C** Soon
   B Tomorrow   **D** Lately

Using Adverbs to Show Time Order

The steps in a how-to explanation should be in the correct order. Use adverbs to tell when to do each step.

- <u>First</u>, pick the potato bugs from the plants.
- <u>Later</u>, pull the weeds out of the dirt.

A Add an adverb from the list to show the order of the steps clearly. Write the paragraph.

> Finally Now First Then

1. _____ place an empty bucket outside. **2.** _____ let the bucket fill up with rainwater for a few days. **3.** _____ when the bucket is almost full, bring it to your garden. **4.** _____ use this recycled water for your plants.

B Arrange these steps in the correct order. Add adverbs such as *next* and *last* to show time order. Add a closing sentence. Write the paragraph.

5. _____ pour water gently on the planted seeds. **6.** _____ collect a flowerpot, some soil, a seed packet, and water. **7.** _____ fill the flowerpot an inch from the top with soil. **8.** _____ sprinkle seeds in the soil and add more soil to cover them. **9.** _____

C Write a set of instructions for an indoor or outdoor activity you enjoy. Use adverbs to put the steps in time order.

Capitalization

A **proper noun** names a particular person, place, or thing. All important words of a proper noun are capitalized. This includes titles and initials.

A **proper adjective** is formed from a proper noun. All important words in proper adjectives are capitalized.

In a letter, all the words of the greeting and the first word of the closing are capitalized.

- <u>Ms</u>. <u>Hitz</u> wrote many stories.
- In one story, an <u>Indian</u> girl named <u>Rani</u> had a clever idea.

A Write the sentences. Capitalize all proper nouns and proper adjectives.

1. mr. and mrs. young went to india.
2. The family flew from california to the city of bombay.
3. Their daughter, jane, couldn't wait to eat indian food.
4. Her father gazed out at the pacific ocean.

Write correctly each group of words that should be capitalized.

5. monday, june 8
6. a city called calcutta
7. striped tigers
8. last week

9. a sunny day
10. a nice bakery
11. dear cousin kumar,
12. mexican food

B Write the sentences. Correct any capitalization mistakes. If a sentence has no capitalization mistakes, write **C** next to it.

1. jan will be visiting london and paris.
2. Her ship will sail on the sixth of May.
3. Jan can't wait to see the famous eiffel tower.
4. Paul, her uncle, will meet her at the dock.
5. He always signs his notes, "love, Uncle Paul."
6. The country of france has been his home for many years.

C Complete each sentence with a word or group of words from the box. Capitalize all proper nouns and proper adjectives. Write the paragraph.

mexican	Fourth of july	main street
ortiz	elmville	juan

7. I live on _____. 8. Mrs. _____ lives next door to us. 9. She and her son, _____, often visit my family. 10. We celebrated the _____ with them. 11. Then they invited us for _____ food. 12. I'm glad they live in _____.

Review and Assess

Write the proper nouns and proper adjectives correctly.

1. The people of stockton were hungry.
2. This small english town had a nasty ruler.
3. Mean prince peter made an announcement in june.
4. "Let the hungry people go across the atlantic ocean!"
5. This story was written by michael stuart.
6. Other stories of his take place in new mexico.

Write the letter of the word or words that should be capitalized.

7. This russian story is about a dancing school.

    A story   C school
    B dancing   D russian

8. Life is odd at the dancing school that mrs. popov owns.

    A mrs. popov   C dancing
    B school   D odd

9. Poor rachel does not want to dance for her aunt.

    A dance   C rachel
    B aunt   D want

10. Horrible cousin dulcie shows off at ballet class.

    A class   C shows
    B ballet   D cousin dulcie

Capitalizing Proper Nouns and Adjectives

When you write, you want to be exact about people and places. Proper nouns and proper adjectives add important details. Capitalize these words correctly so readers are not confused.

- My collection has <u>Spanish</u> dolls from <u>Aunt Rosa</u> in <u>Madrid</u>.

A This paragraph has some capitalization errors. Correct the errors. Then add a closing sentence. Write the paragraph.

1. Starting a doll collection is easy. **2.** There are lovely dolls from france and japan at garage sales. **3.** Dolls from germany and china are also popular. **4.** You could collect raggedy ann dolls too. **5.** My friend marta and I go to doll shows that advertise in the seattle newspapers. **6.** _____

B Add your own proper nouns or proper adjectives to complete the sentences.

7. You do not have to be from _____ to cook great pasta. **8.** Aunt _____ says that anyone can fix good pasta. **9.** When I visited her in _____, I watched her drop noodles into boiling water. **10.** She used a brand called _____ Pasta, but any spaghetti will do. **11.** Once I learn how to make perfect pasta, I will open a restaurant called _____.

C Write a paragraph that tells how you might plan a vacation. Tell where you would go, what sights you could see, and who would go with you.

Contractions

A **contraction** is a word made by putting two words together.
An **apostrophe (')** shows where letters have been left out.
Pronouns can be used with the verbs *am, is, are, have, has, had,* and
will to make contractions. Some contractions are formed by
putting a verb with the word *not*. Below are some examples.

Pronoun and verb: she + will = she'll   I + am = I'm
we + have = we've it + is = it's
he + would = he'd   they + are = they're

Verb and *not*: do + not = don't   have + not = haven't
did + not = didn't   will + not = won't

 A Write the sentences. Underline the contractions.

1. Folk tales usually aren't true.
2. The people in them didn't really exist.
3. Still, we'll learn a lot from reading these tales.
4. We'd like to read a folk tale about wishes coming true.

Write each contraction. Then write the words that make up
the contraction.

5. I'll share some of my favorite folk tales with you.
6. You've got to read this one about a happy bear.
7. A girl can't help but like the friendly bear.
8. One day, she cries because he isn't there.

B Write a contraction to replace the underlined words.

1. <u>I have</u> read an interesting story.
2. <u>It is</u> a legend about a Native American girl.
3. <u>You will</u> enjoy the tale too.
4. Some wicked sisters tease a girl until <u>she is</u> miserable.
5. Now <u>they have</u> learned that she is a true princess.
6. <u>She will</u> forgive them because she is so kind.

C Match the pair of words on the left with the contraction on the right.

7. does not
8. I will
9. he has
10. we have
11. will not
12. she is
13. I would
14. they are
15. do not

a. he's
b. won't
c. she's
d. doesn't
e. I'll
f. we've
g. they're
h. don't
i. I'd

Review and Assess

Write the sentences. Replace the underlined words with a contraction.

1. <u>We have</u> learned about many traditions this year.
2. <u>You will</u> remember how people lived long ago.
3. <u>They had</u> trusted the Earth to give them food.
4. Life <u>was not</u> all hard work, though.
5. People <u>could not</u> be happy without celebrations.

Write the letter of the correct contraction for the underlined words.

6. Cinderella <u>was not</u> always a poor, unhappy girl.

    A weren't   **C** wasnot'
    B wasn't   **D** won't

7. Her stepsisters <u>were not</u> very nice to her.

    A hadn't   **C** weren't
    B we're   **D** wasn't

8. <u>I will</u> bet you know how her story ends.

    A I'll   **C** I'd
    B I'm   **D** Ill'

9. <u>She is</u> going to marry a kind-hearted prince.

    A She'd   **C** She'll
    B It's   **D** She's

Using Contractions in Your Writing

Contractions make writing sound more natural to your readers. Remember to use an apostrophe (') where letters are left out.

A Put these how-to sentences in order. Then replace the underlined words with contractions. Write the paragraph.

Row, Row, Row!

1. Next, make sure the oars are locked onto the boat.
2. At last, <u>you will</u> see how much fun it is to row a boat.
3. Second, be sure <u>you are</u> sitting in the center of the seat.
4. Now <u>do not</u> pull one oar harder than the other or you will go in circles! **5.** First, have an adult help you into the rowboat.

B Add a contraction to this list for planning a party. Write the sentences. The first one is done for you.

6. We'll have a party on Saturday.
7. _____ write the invitations.
8. _____ already made party favors.
9. _____ going to be a sunny day.
10. _____ asked my parents to set up tables.
11. _____ done a good job planning the fun.

C Write a report that tells how you and your classmates planned a special event. Use contractions for a natural style.

Writing a How-to Report

A **test** may ask you to write a how-to report. Remember to include all the steps. Use words such as *first* and *next* to help order the steps. Follow the tips below.

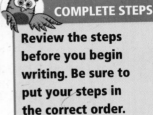

COMPLETE STEPS

Review the steps before you begin writing. Be sure to put your steps in the correct order.

Understand the prompt. Make sure you know what to do. Read the prompt carefully. A prompt for a how-to report could look like this:

> **Write a report that gives steps on how to make or do something. Make your report interesting to read and easy to understand. Explain all the steps and materials needed.**

Key words and phrases are *steps, how to make or do something,* and *materials.*

Find a good topic. Choose an activity you can do well and easily. Think about hobbies such as crafts, sports, or cooking.

Organize your ideas. Create a how-to chart. Write the name of the task, the materials needed, an introduction, a list of steps, and an ending. A list of steps might look like the one below.

Steps:	Find a large, flat piece of driftwood or a board.
	Gather interesting objects from the beach.
	Let objects dry completely.
	Arrange objects on the board.
	Glue objects to the board.

Write a good beginning. Write a strong opening sentence that tells readers what you are about to explain.

Develop and elaborate ideas. Use your chart to help you organize your ideas clearly. Remember to use order words.

Write a strong ending. Use the ending to sum up your explanation.

Check your work. Read your report and make any needed changes.

See how the how-to report below answers the prompt, has a strong beginning and ending, and puts steps in a clear order.

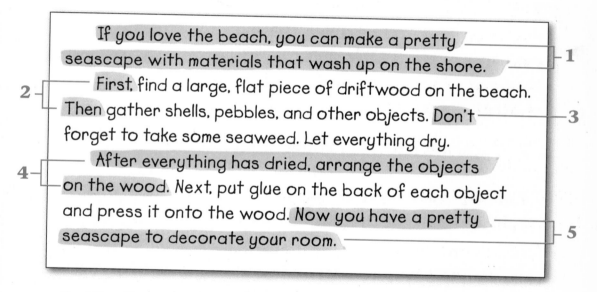

1. The first sentence tells what the task will be.
2. The writer uses words that show the order of steps.
3. A contraction makes the report sound natural.
4. The steps are in an order that makes sense.
5. The ending sums up the explanation.

Pronouns

A **noun** names a person, place, or thing. A **pronoun** takes the place of one or more nouns. A **singular pronoun** takes the place of a singular noun. A **plural pronoun** takes the place of a plural noun or of more than one noun. The pronoun *I* is always capitalized.

Singular Pronouns				Plural Pronouns			
I	you	he	she	we	they	us	them
it	me	him	her	you			

- **I** visited Aunt Jean and Uncle Jim. **They** made **me** feel welcome.

A Write the pronoun in each sentence.

1. Uncle Jim told me an interesting story.
2. He piloted a plane from California to China.
3. The passengers and crew members depended on him.
4. They knew the flight would be long and tiring.

Write **S** if the underlined pronoun is singular.
Write **P** if it is plural.

5. <u>We</u> took an exciting plane trip.
6. My seat was big, and <u>it</u> reclined.
7. <u>I</u> watched the clouds float by the little window.
8. The pilot showed <u>me</u> around the cockpit.

B Match each word or group of words on the left with a pronoun on the right. Write the pronouns.

1. an airplane   we
2. my mom   he
3. the dark clouds   it
4. Dad   they
5. Aunt Jean and I   she

C Write the pronoun that replaces the underlined words.

6. The pilots flew through the dark night.
7. The Earth seemed very distant to the man.
8. Most people were asleep at that hour.
9. You and I would have been safe in bed.
10. His destination was thousands of miles away.
11. He looked down at the Hawaiian Islands.
12. Mountains and beaches dotted the ocean.
13. The water sparkled around the beach.
14. He described the landing for you and me.
15. As the passengers left, they thanked the crew.

Review and Assess

Write the pronoun in each sentence.

1. We are reading about flying in the 1920s.
2. Have you ever heard of barnstormers?
3. They were pilots traveling around the country.
4. People paid them for rides and flying lessons.
5. Some of them did dangerous tricks on the planes.
6. I want to read more about barnstormers.

Read each sentence. Write the letter of the word that can replace the underlined word or group of words.

7. Linda is studying <u>the Wright brothers</u>.

   A him   **C** her

   B them   **D** it

8. <u>These inventors</u> made a simple airplane.

   A It   **C** They

   B Her   **D** He

9. <u>An early plane</u> could carry only one person.

   A Him   **C** They

   B It   **D** He

10. <u>Linda</u> says the brothers were very brave.

    A He   **C** They

    B It   **D** She

Using Pronouns in Your Writing

When some words are repeated too often, your writing becomes wordy and boring. Use pronouns to keep your readers interested.

- Airplanes were made of cloth, but now <u>airplanes</u> are metal.
- Airplanes were made of cloth, but now <u>they</u> are metal.

A Replace the underlined words with these pronouns. Write the sentences. Capitalize words correctly.

> they   she   it   he   we

1. Kate read a book by Jim Day that <u>Kate</u> bought.
2. <u>The book</u> is about Orville and Wilbur Wright.
3. <u>Orville and Wilbur Wright</u> flew their plane from Kitty Hawk.
4. <u>Kate and I and our classmates</u> think the book is interesting.
5. The author loves airplanes, and <u>the author</u> flies them too.

B Make these sentences less wordy. Replace some repeated words with pronouns. Write the new paragraph.

    6. My favorite artist is Claude Monet. I read several books about Claude Monet. **7.** He loved light and the way light looks in different places. **8.** One of his paintings of water lilies shows water lilies in a pond. **9.** Monet's colors are soft, but often colors can be quite strong.

C Write a short report about a class project such as a mural. Use pronouns to keep your reader's interest.

Subject and Object Pronouns

Pronouns can take the place of words in the subject of a sentence. These pronouns are **subject pronouns.**

> <u>I</u> watch ducklings in the park.   <u>They</u> make us laugh.

Pronouns can take the place of words in the predicate of a sentence. These pronouns are **object pronouns.**

> The ducks entertain <u>us</u>.   I bring bread for <u>them</u>.

Subject Pronouns				**Object Pronouns**			
I	you	he	she	me	you	him	her
it	we	they		it	us	them	

 Read the sentences. Write all the pronouns.

1. Oka-san brings the ducklings to the pool with her.
2. She has lined them up.
3. We think they are cute.
4. Do you see that man?
5. He is a photographer.
6. I posed with the ducks.
7. They quacked loudly.
8. Oka-san posed with us too.

B Read each sentence. Write all the subject pronouns in one column. Write all the object pronouns in another column.

1. You can see different kinds of animals in the city.
2. Wild birds and creatures interest us.
3. We will photograph them in the park.
4. The park guide will help us with the project.
5. She knows many things about animal habits.
6. I will ask her about bats too.
7. Mark told me about raccoons and foxes.
8. They live in the woods near the park.

C Correct the underlined subject and object pronouns. Write the paragraph.

9. <u>Us</u> saw a nature film yesterday. 10. The film explained a lot to <u>we</u> about animal behavior. 11. You and <u>me</u> sleep while some animals are awake. 12. <u>Me</u> asked the teacher what those animals do at night. 13. <u>Her</u> says that nighttime is hunting time. 14. <u>Them</u> can see very well in the dark. 15. The film showed <u>they</u> finding food. 16. Alain asked <u>she</u> for another film about animals.

Review and Assess

Write the sentences. Underline the pronouns. Write **SP** for a subject pronoun or **OP** for an object pronoun.

1. We can learn many things from animals.
2. They take care of offspring, just as people do.
3. Mothers teach them to hunt for food.
4. Lena's kitten taught us how to find a mouse!

Read the paragraph. Write the letter of the word that should replace the underlined word or words.

5. Anik gave a good book to <u>Dan and I</u>. 6. <u>Us</u> read the book aloud together. 7. That was fun for <u>we</u> to do on a rainy day. 8. I like Anik because <u>her</u> is interested in so many things.

5. **A** I   **C** they
      B them   **D** us

6. **A** Him   **C** We
      B Her   **D** Them

7. **A** us   **C** he
      B she   **D** I

8. **A** him   **C** me
      B she   **D** it

Writing with Subject and Object Pronouns

Pronouns are handy tools for smoothing out a report. Use pronouns correctly to make your writing clear.

- Jay and I learned about ducks. He gave me a book about them.

A Make each sentence clear. Use the pronouns below correctly. Write the sentences.

him   It   me   she   they

1. Mrs. Parks is the best librarian because _____ chooses wonderful books. **2.** I asked her to choose a book for _____. **3.** _____ was about a girl mouse with a new brother. **4.** The girl did not like _____. **5.** Finally, _____ became friends.

B Use the kind of pronoun in ( ) to complete each sentence. Then add a final sentence to complete the paragraph.

6. (subject pronoun) learned that a mother lion is protective of her cubs. **7.** She roars loudly to keep enemies from attacking (object pronoun). **8.** It surprised (object pronoun) that females can be fiercer than males. **9.** If you want to learn more about lions, _____.

C Write a paragraph about an important person who has visited your classroom. Use pronouns to keep your writing smooth and clear.

Possessive Pronouns

Possessive pronouns can show who or what owns, or possesses, something.

Singular possessive pronouns

   my/mine   your/yours   her/hers   his   its

- Jen and I both have sleds.
  <u>Her</u> sled is bright orange. <u>Mine</u> is dark blue.

Plural possessive pronouns

   our/ours   your/yours   their/theirs

- My boots are heavy.
  <u>Their</u> soles are thick. Are these boots <u>yours</u>?

A Write the possessive pronoun in each sentence.

   1. The wind lashed the explorers with its huge gusts.
   2. Their hands and feet were frozen.
   3. Yours would have been too!

Read the paragraph. Write all the possessive pronouns.

   4. My favorite movie characters are brave girls. **5.** Are yours heroines too? **6.** Their courage is amazing! **7.** Let's share our favorite movie characters. **8.** Takia says hers is a character named Matilda. **9.** Mine is Heidi. **10.** Ours are both brave girls who looked trouble right in the face.

B Write the possessive pronoun in ( ) that could replace the underlined words.

1. I admire <u>the women's</u> courage. (his, their)
2. Your fear is bugs, but <u>my fear</u> is lightning. (mine, its)
3. Lisa wrote a story about <u>John's</u> adventure. (his, ours)
4. These tickets are for <u>Sam's and my</u> trip. (mine, our)
5. Is this map <u>the map you own</u>? (its, yours)
6. The suitcase is heavy for <u>the suitcase's</u> size. (ours, its)

C Write the possessive pronoun that takes the place of each underlined word or words.

7. Gram was sick so we did <u>Gram's</u> chores.
8. <u>Tim's and my</u> next job was to dust all the bookshelves.
9. <u>The house's</u> floors were tracked with mud.
10. The hardest task was <u>Gramps's</u>.
11. Gramps had to milk <u>Gram and Gramps's</u> cows.
12. The milking stool wobbled on <u>the milking stool's</u> legs.
13. Tim and I were glad that the milking job was not <u>Tim's and my job</u>!

Review and Assess

Write the possessive pronouns in each sentence.

1. My family lives in the mountains.
2. Our area gets tons of snow.
3. Laura's house is next to mine.
4. Laura brings her sled to my yard.
5. Ours has a steep hill for sledding.

Write the letter of the possessive pronoun that best completes each sentence.

6. I bring _____ crafts project to school.

   A mine   **C** my
   B yours   **D** hers

7. The teacher told us all to remember _____ materials.

   A hers   **C** mine
   B ours   **D** our

8. My parents could use a tablecloth for _____ table.

   A their   **C** theirs
   B her   **D** mine

9. _____ will be a pretty one with red and white checks.

   A My   **C** Its
   B Theirs   **D** Our

Using Possessive Pronouns in Your Writing

When you write, use possessive pronouns to show who or what owns something in a clear, simple way. Your writing will be easier to read.

- Mr. James drives <u>Mr. James's</u> snowplow over the roads.
- Mr. James drives <u>his</u> snowplow over the roads.

A Make these sentences less wordy. Replace the underlined words with a word or words from the list below. Write the sentences.

    My next report   their   Their boards   My family

  1. <u>The family I live with</u> likes to sled in winter.
  2. Some people build <u>some people's</u> own sleds.
  3. <u>The boards of the sleds</u> come from recycled wood.
  4. <u>The next report that I write</u> will be about homemade sleds.

B Correct the pronoun errors with possessive pronouns. Then add a closing sentence of your own. Write the paragraph.

    5. The cold air is heading toward <u>us</u> town.
6. Thick clouds gather over <u>me</u> street. **7.** What makes clouds drop <u>they</u> ice crystals, or snowflakes? **8.** When the crystals get too big and heavy, snow falls on <u>us</u> heads!
9. _____

C Write a paragraph about preparing for a storm. Use possessive pronouns correctly.

Prepositions

A **preposition** is the first word in a **prepositional phrase.**

- The newspaperman read <u>to</u> everyone.

The **object of the preposition** is the noun or pronoun that follows it. The preposition shows a relationship between the noun or pronoun and another word or words in a sentence.

- Booker held the book <u>with care</u>. (how)
- <u>At night,</u> he tried to read. (when)
- Booker saw the letters <u>on the page</u>. (where)

Common Prepositions

after	at	before	behind	by	down	for
from	in	near	of	on	to	with

A Write the preposition in each sentence.

1. Booker T. Washington was born in Virginia.
2. He was the child of a poor family.
3. After the Civil War, the family became free.
4. Booker learned the alphabet from a book.
5. Young Booker became famous for his knowledge.
6. Reading is important to me as well.
7. Have you read about Booker T. Washington?
8. This book was in the library.

B Write the prepositional phrase in each sentence.
Circle the preposition.

1. Before the Civil War, things were very different.
2. Slaves lived under cruel laws. **3.** In those days, they could not attend school. **4.** Some learned the alphabet from other people. **5.** With this new knowledge, the slaves felt freer. **6.** Later, schools were open to everyone.

C Choose a preposition from the box that makes sense in each sentence. Write the sentences.

about	during	onto	to	inside

7. I have a book _____ schools and education long ago.
8. The book has information that is interesting _____ me.
9. Students studied _____ a one-room schoolhouse.
10. They sat near a wood stove _____ cold winter days.
11. The students copied their lessons _____ small slates.

Review and Assess

Write the sentences. Underline the preposition in each sentence.

1. Should I borrow some books from the library?
2. The librarian is always helpful to me.
3. She knows I enjoy books about nature.
4. I notice two good books on the shelf.

Read the sentences. Write the letter of the word that is a preposition.

5. I admire people who are helpful with others.

   A offer   **C** with
   B who   **D** people

6. Heroes don't just think of themselves.

   A of   **C** just
   B themselves   **D** think

7. They use their abilities in many ways.

   A use   **C** many
   B in   **D** their

8. These good people should be rewarded for their work.

   A good   **C** for
   B should   **D** their

Adding Details to Your Writing

Prepositional phrases add information to reports and make your meaning clear. Use prepositional phrases to include important details.

- I enjoy reading.   I enjoy reading <u>about American history</u>.

A Choose a preposition from the box to complete each sentence. Finish the last sentence with a prepositional phrase of your own. Write the paragraph.

about	in	from

1. There are hundreds of books stacked _____ our library. **2.** Some are stories that tell _____ famous people. **3.** Others have pictures _____ long ago. **4.** Someday, you might read a biography _____!

B Add a prepositional phrase of your own to complete each sentence. Then write a closing sentence. Write the paragraph.

5. I am writing a report _____. **6.** Most of my facts will come _____. **7.** I will also look _____. **8.** In my report, I will tell _____. **9.** _____

C Write a short report about a person who has done something special for others. Use prepositional phrases to add details.

Conjunctions

A **conjunction** connects words or groups of words. Three common conjunctions are *and, but,* and *or.* Add a comma before the conjunction when you connect complete sentences.

To add information, use *and:* The weather is hot <u>and</u> dry.
To show a choice, use *or:* We must sell the chickens <u>or</u> the pigs.
To show a difference, use *but:* We hope it will rain, <u>but</u> it hasn't yet.

A Write the conjunction in each sentence.

1. Dad drives the truck or the tractor.
2. I am small but strong.
3. I want to help, and Dad lets me.
4. We can pick corn first or clean the pens.
5. I'd work all day, but we have to stop for lunch.

Choose the conjunction in ( ) that best completes each sentence. Write the sentence.

6. Mom served pork and beans, (or, and) I ate a lot!
7. Should I wash the pails (but, or) rake the hay?
8. We went into the barn, (or, and) I groomed the horses.
9. Our day was busy, (but, or) I didn't mind.

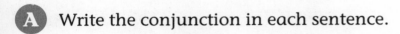

B Choose *and, or,* or *but* to complete each sentence.
Write the conjunction.

1. Do you like the city _____ the country better?
2. Dad loves farm life, _____ Mom misses the city.
3. She likes busy streets _____ many people.
4. I like my apartment, _____ I love this great farm!
5. I'll either be a farmer _____ a rancher.

C Match the words on the left with a word or words on the right.
Join them with *and, or,* or *but* to make a complete sentence.
Write each sentence.

6. During a drought, it's hot   not August.
7. People hope for rain   red.
8. I like June   dry.
9. I am sunburned   cooler weather.
10. Farmer Hal grows corn   wheat.
11. Is that thunder   close the windows.
12. Run inside   loud music?

Review and Assess

Write each sentence with *and, or,* or *but.*

1. Children _____ parents can help each other.
2. Either Susie _____ I do the chores.
3. We can help, _____ our brother is too young for chores.
4. Mom helps with homework _____ drives us to school.
5. Some families argue, _____ we get along very well.

Write the letter of the group of words that best completes each sentence.

6. Horses are big, but _____

   A tall animals.   C ponies are small.
   B Jim is afraid.   D can't ride one.

7. Are these bulls, or _____

   A are they cows?   C I like cows too.
   B we raise pigs.   D neither does Sam.

8. I enjoy the country, but _____

   A our farm.   C the fresh air.
   B city life is fun too. D you do.

9. I'm getting strong, but _____

   A I have muscles.   C hard work.
   B lift heavy pails.   D Dad is stronger.

Using Conjunctions in Your Writing

Too many short sentences can make your writing sound choppy.
Use *and, or,* or *but* to combine words or sentences for a smooth style.

- My dad grew up on a farm. My uncle grew up on a farm.
- <u>My Dad and my uncle</u> grew up on a farm.

A Use a conjunction to complete each sentence.

1. Many years ago, the land was dry _____ dusty.
2. People tried to save their farms, _____ they had to move
away. **3.** Did they travel west _____ east? **4.** Many people
went to California _____ Oregon. **5.** The trip was long
_____ difficult.

B Use *and, or,* or *but* to combine each pair of short sentences.
Use a comma to connect two complete sentences. Then add
a closing sentence. Write the paragraph.

6. Farmers are important to our state. They help our
whole country. **7.** Some farms are very large. Others are small.
8. The fruits and vegetables must be shipped quickly. They will
spoil. **9.** Most farmers love farming. Their work is very hard.
10. _____

C Write a report about workers in your school. Keep your writing
smooth by using conjunctions to join choppy sentences.

Writing a Summary

Some **tests** may ask you to write a summary from a graph, time line, or chart. You will need to read the information carefully and use it in your own sentences. Follow the tips below.

FACT SHEETS

Fact sheets list important information about a topic, usually on one page. To summarize these facts, use them in smooth, complete sentences and create paragraphs.

Organize your ideas. You will need to decide how to present the facts. Think about which facts you want to use first and which you will save until the end.

Write a good beginning. Get your reader's attention. Think of a topic sentence that presents the main idea clearly.

FACT SHEET ABOUT DRAGONFLIES

When they first appeared
- Millions of years ago for some species
- Older than the dinosaurs

What they look like
- Long body, two pairs of glittering wings
- Different sizes

Where they live
- Anywhere except very cold areas
- Many in hot climates

How they move
- Strong fliers

What they eat
- Small insects of every kind, including mosquitoes

Develop and elaborate ideas. Include facts from your fact sheet that support your main idea.

Write a strong ending. Write sentences that pull the information together. You might also add your feelings about the topic.

Check your work. See if you need to add any information.

See how the summary below uses the information from the fact sheet, along with the writer's own ideas and sentences.

<u>Amazing Dragonflies</u>

Which creature is older than the dinosaur? ——— 1

2 [Dragonflies are beautiful insects that have survived for millions of years. A dragonfly is about two inches long.

This insect is also unusual because it has two pairs ——— 3
of wings that glitter on its long body. The dragonfly's strong wings make it a good flier. Dragonflies can live ——— 4
almost anywhere. Many types live in the tropics. They all eat mosquitoes and other small insects. Since dragonflies can live and feed almost anywhere, they will probably ——— 5
survive for a long time to come.

1. The opening question grabs the reader's attention.
2. This sentence states the main idea.
3. Pronouns avoid repeating words.
4. The writer adds more about a fact.
5. The ending pulls facts together and shows the writer's idea.

Review of Sentences

A **sentence** is a group of words that tells, asks, commands, or exclaims something. A sentence must express a complete thought. It begins with a capital letter and ends with an end mark.

Sentence: I would like to have a piñata at my party.

Not a sentence: A piñata at my party.

A Read each group of words. Write **S** if it is a complete sentence. Write **NS** if it is not a complete sentence.

1. To make a piñata in my family.
2. Many different shapes and sizes.
3. We choose a different shape for every party.
4. A hollow center.
5. Piñatas are filled with treats.
6. Isn't it fun to make piñatas?

Read the groups of words. Write the complete sentence in each pair.

7. Planned a surprise party. We planned a surprise party.
8. We baked such a tasty cake. Such a tasty cake.
9. Blew up balloons. Dad and I blew up balloons.
10. So many balloons. I had never seen so many balloons!

B Choose the group of words in ( ) that will complete each sentence. Write the complete sentence.

1. My brother Rick _____ (to plan parties, plans parties).
2. His parties _____ (having fun, are wonderful)!
3. Rick likes to _____ (delight children, the best ideas).
4. His handmade piñatas _____ (large pole, are popular).
5. The games he organizes (are great fun, and fun too).
6. Every party guest _____ (a gift, wins a prize).

C Add your own words to each group of words to make a complete sentence. Write the sentences.

7. a game called Pin the Tail on the Donkey
8. covered my eyes
9. took the paper tail
10. blindfold
11. walked carefully
12. whispering in the room
13. toward the donkey
14. pinned the tail on its ear

Review and Assess

Read each group of words. Write **S** if it is a sentence.
Write **NS** if it is not a sentence.

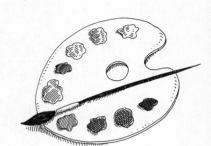

1. Making party favors with my guests.
2. Everyone likes the monster puppets.
3. Old socks, buttons, and pipe cleaners.
4. This is the arts and crafts table.
5. Can we use glitter too?
6. Cardboard for the hands.

Read the paragraph. Write the letter of the words that
can complete each sentence correctly.

7. Making crafts _____ **8.** I _____ **9.** _____ collage of
paper and fabric. **10.** _____ fun in the art room.

7. A is so much fun.   **C** is so much.
    B so much.   **D** much fun.

8. A pictures.   **C** make pictures.
    B crafting.   **D** making pictures.

9. A It's a collage   **C** Nice
    B Large   **D** Look at this

10. A Always   **C** Crafting
     B We always have   **D** Collage

Using Different Sentences to Add Style

Writers use different kinds of sentences to persuade their readers and keep them interested. Statements, questions, commands, and exclamations add style to your writing.

- Look around at our city parks. Piles of trash cover the fresh, green grass. How can we clean up our parks?

A Change each underlined sentence to the kind of sentence in ( ).

1. <u>Students can help keep the schoolyard clean.</u> (question) **2.** Litter and weeds make our school look messy. **3.** We should pull weeds and pick up trash. **4.** <u>People could volunteer this week.</u> (command) **5.** <u>We could make a difference</u>. (exclamation) **6.** Then we would have a clean place to play at recess.

B Tell about a job that needs to be done in your town. Complete these sentences with your own ideas.

7. This spring, we should _____.
8. Wouldn't you like to _____?
9. Make this a better place to live by _____.
10. What a great _____!

C Write four sentences for a poster that persuades students to do a clean-up job in your neighborhood. Use different types of sentences to keep your readers interested.

Compound Sentences

Two simple sentences can be combined into a **compound sentence.** Use a comma and a conjunction such as *and, but,* or *or* to join the sentences. Begin the second sentence with a small letter unless the first word is a proper noun, a proper adjective, or the pronoun *I.*

We bought our tickets. Soon we boarded the ship.
We bought our tickets, and soon we boarded the ship.

A Write **S** if the sentence is a simple sentence.
Write **C** if the sentence is a compound sentence.

1. Let's take a vacation soon.
2. I want to fly to Boston, but Mom wants to drive.
3. This will be my first trip on a plane.
4. It's almost April now, and I will travel then.
5. I am eager to go, and I have packed my bag.

Choose one of the words in ( ) to combine these simple sentences. Write the compound sentences.

6. My cousin Liz lives in Boston. I live in New York. (but, or)
7. Spring vacation is here. I am taking a trip. (and, or)
8. The plane is full. I find my seat easily. (but, or)
9. Does the trip seem very long? Am I just bored? (but, or)

B Use the conjunctions *and, but,* or *or* to combine each pair of sentences. Write the compound sentence.

1. Long ago, travel was hard. People did not visit often.
2. People rode horses. Sometimes they walked.
3. Now there are planes and trains. Traveling is easier.
4. Cars go fast. Planes go even faster.
5. Dad drives. I read the map.

C Read each sentence in the paragraph below. Add a sentence from the box and a conjunction to form a compound sentence. Write the paragraph.

> It grazes in the grass.   We hear the frogs croak.
> It hops away.   You can enjoy them.
> We search for different animals outside.

6. We look through the car window _____. 7. There is a deer _____. 8. We drive by a pond _____. 9. Up pops a rabbit _____. 10. Car rides can be long _____.

Review and Assess

Combine these short sentences with a comma and the word *and* to form a compound sentence.

1. I want to drive a car. Dad will teach me one day.
2. He is a driving teacher. He has many students.
3. We live in the country. Everyone drives a truck.
4. Mom delivers mail. She drives a truck too.
5. We live near a big road. We hear the noisy traffic.

Write the letter of the words that complete the sentence correctly.

6. We always bring food on a _____ pack fruit and cheese.

A trip, and I	**C** trip, And I
B trip. And I	**D** trip and I

7. It is warm _____ packs our sweaters anyway.

A today, But Mom	**C** today but Mom
B today. but Mom	**D** today, but Mom

8. I like fresh _____ open windows make a nice breeze.

A air, and the	**C** air, And the
B air, and The	**D** air. and The

9. Mom points to a _____ turns off the highway.

A sign. And Dad	**C** sign, and Dad
B sign, And Dad	**D** sign. and Dad

Combining Sentences to Improve Your Style

Sentence combining is one way to make your persuasive letter read smoothly. Join sentences with *and, or,* or *but.*

- Camp is fun. I can't wait to go.
  Camp is fun, and I can't wait to go.

A Use the word in ( ) to combine each pair of choppy sentences. Remember to add a comma. Write the paragraph.

1. Summer days are long. I get bored. (and) **2.** I have some ideas. I told Mom about them. (and) **3.** I could play in the yard. I could visit my friend Cindy. (or) **4.** It's fun to play outside. I miss Cindy. (but) **5.** Her family lives in Salem. They invited me for a visit. (and) **6.** I'll tell this to Mom. Maybe she'll let me take the trip. (and)

B Combine each pair of short sentences. Write a sentence to end the letter. Write the letter and sign it.

Dear Rachel,

7. Camp is fun. I miss you. **8.** My cabin is cozy. I made new friends. **9.** I usually take arts and crafts. Sometimes I play ball. **10.** There is a cookout at night. We toast marshmallows. **11.** _____

C Write a letter persuading a friend to join a club or go to camp. Combine short sentences for a smooth style. Use *and, or,* or *but.*

Commas

Use a **comma** and a conjunction to join two complete sentences.

The girls had to cook, <u>and</u> they were scared.

Use commas to separate words in a series.

They made <u>chicken, cornbread, and carrots</u> for dinner.

Commas are also used to separate the month and the day from the year, and to separate the year from the rest of the sentence.

On <u>December 14, 2005,</u> our winter break begins.

A comma is used after both the greeting and the closing of a friendly letter.

Dear Theo,   Your friend, Sandy

Use a comma between the names of a street, city, and state abbreviation in an address and after the name of a city and a state in a sentence. Don't use a comma between a state abbreviation and a ZIP code.

Julio moved to Portland, Maine, last year.
I live at 123 West Elm <u>Street, New York, NY</u> 10024.

A Write **C** if commas are used correctly. Write **NC** if commas are not used correctly.

1. Cooking class is starting, and all students are welcome.
2. Send this to 166 Woodmont Road Berkeley CA 94708.
3. Learn about cooking, baking, and serving food.

B Find the comma errors in these sentences.
Write each sentence using correct punctuation.

1. June 25 2002, is a day I will always remember.
2. My mother aunt, and I went to Italy.
3. I left my baby brother cat, and dog at home.
4. We eat all kinds of food but we love Italian food.
5. I sampled spaghetti, pizza and pastries in Italy.
6. We enjoyed the shops, outdoor markets and cafés.
7. Mom brought recipes back home to Toledo Ohio.
8. She is a chef and our family certainly likes to cook!

C Write each sentence. Add commas where they are needed.

9. I visited Boston and I saw some of the famous sights.
10. The Boston Tea Party was on December 16 1773.
11. It happened in Boston Massachusetts.
12. It wasn't a party and nobody drank tea!
13. Americans paid too much for coffee spices and tea.
14. They threw tea overboard and they defied the king.

Review and Assess

Write each sentence. Add commas where they are needed.

1. On December 24 2002 I made a huge fruitcake.
2. I put in nuts dates and candied fruit.
3. It was my first homemade cake and I was proud.
4. We had just moved to Scranton Pennsylvania.
5. Dad took a picture of the cake and we all ate some.

Read the paragraph below. Then write the letter of the rule for comma use to correct each error.

6. Dear Asa

7. We ate at my uncle's restaurant and everyone had a great meal. **8.** We enjoyed tacos chili and rice. **9.** The address is 1200 Lake Drive Coppell Texas.

6. **A** (,) in a series   **C** (,) to join sentences
   B (,) in a greeting   **D** (,) in an address

7. **A** (,) in a series   **C** (,) to join sentences
   B (,) in a date   **D** (,) in an address

8. **A** (,) in a series   **C** (,) to join sentences
   B (,) in a date   **D** (,) in an address

9. **A** (,) in a series   **C** (,) to join sentences
   B (,) in a date   **D** (,) in an address

Using Commas in Your Writing

You want to have clear sentences in your persuasive letter. When you list reasons and facts or join sentences, use commas correctly.

- You'll love this cookbook because it's handy, interesting, and easy to read.

A Make the information clear by adding commas. Write the paragraph.

> **1.** Our cookbook will be published on July 18 2005. **2.** It has healthful recipes and readers will love them. **3.** Our recipes call for vegetables grains and fruits. **4.** Order a copy from 14 Halsey Place Clark PA 18098. **5.** You won't be disappointed with our recipes for breads pastas and desserts.

B Complete each sentence with your own words. Use commas to keep your sentences clear.

> **6.** I live at _____ (number and street) in _____ (city and state).
> **7.** I was born on _____ (day) _____ (year).
> **8.** My favorite foods are _____ _____ and _____.
> **9.** My favorite games are _____ _____ and _____.

C Use some of the sentences above in a letter. Persuade a friend to come to your house for a party. Use commas correctly.

Quotations

Quotation marks show the exact words of a speaker. Use a comma to separate the words in **quotations** from the rest of the sentence. Begin a quotation with a capital letter. Put the end punctuation mark inside the quotation marks.

"The boat launch will be exciting," Bob said.
"When will it take place?" I asked.
Bob shouted, "In less than an hour!"

 A Write the part of the sentence that is a quotation.

1. "Let's build a spaceship," Jennie said.
2. "That's a good idea," Tariq replied.
3. Mom said, "You can use this big box."
4. "Yes, that will be perfect," Jennie agreed.

Write the sentences. Add a comma and quotation marks where they are needed.

5. I want to have an exciting job some day I said.
6. Dad replied This book will give you some good ideas.
7. I want to see it too my little brother said.
8. Children, remember to share Dad told us.
9. I'd like to drive a train my brother cried.
10. Mom said I'm sure you'll both have exciting jobs.

B Write the sentences. Add quotation marks, commas, and other punctuation marks as needed.

1. Do you know what NASA is Eddie asked.
2. It's a big space center Jean told him.
3. What do they do there Eddie asked.
4. They direct the space program Jean explained.
5. Eddie exclaimed Wow, that's fantastic
6. My uncle was an astronaut Jean said.
7. He would be glad to tell you all about it she added.
8. When can we meet him Eddie asked excitedly.

C Write **C** if a sentence is correct. If it is not correct, write the sentence and make the corrections that are needed.

9. "What is gravity?" Sue asked.
10. Mrs. Blake replied It is a force of nature.
11. Would you explain that Sue requested.
12. It is the pull between two objects Mrs. Blake said.
13. Pete added, "Gravity keeps us on Earth."
14. Sue exclaimed Otherwise, we would all float away

Review and Assess

Write the sentences. Add quotation marks, commas, and any other punctuation marks that are needed.

1. What are you drawing Yoko asked.
2. Ann replied I am drawing myself.
3. That is not how you look Yoko exclaimed.
4. This is the way I see myself Ann told her.
5. Do you see yourself as a mermaid Yoko wondered.

Write the letter of the words that should go inside quotation marks.

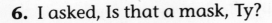

6. I asked, Is that a mask, Ty?

   A Is that a mask, Ty?   **C** I asked
   B I asked, Is   **D** a mask,

7. Yes, do you want to see it? he asked me.

   A Yes, do you   **C** he asked me
   B Yes, do you want to see it?   **D** see it, he

8. I'll try it on, I said.

   A I said   **C** try it on,
   B I'll try   **D** I'll try it on,

9. Ty smiled and said, That's fine.

   A Ty smiled   **C** That's fine.
   B said, That's fine.   **D** smiled

Using Quotations to Support Your Ideas

Quotations can support your persuasive writing.

- I asked Gramps for a kitten. Mr. Leeds, the pet store owner, said, "This kitten will be a great pet. He is calm and quiet."

A Choose a quotation from the box to complete each sentence. Write the paragraph.

> "Caring for pets builds responsibility."
> "I think I should get a cat."
> "Do you think you can care for it?"
> "Amy is ready to have a pet."

1. I told Gramps, _____ **2.** Gramps asked, _____ **3.** Mr. Leeds explained, _____ **4.** Mom added, _____

B Add quotation marks to each sentence. Then add a closing quotation of your own. Write the paragraph.

5. Some older people need help walking their dogs, the police chief said. **6.** We need volunteers for this, said the mayor. **7.** There will be a special dinner for all the helpers, he added. **8.** _____

C Write a short speech persuading friends to help out in your community. Use quotations to support your argument.

Subject-Verb Agreement

The subject and verb in a sentence must work together, or **agree**. To make most present-tense verbs agree with singular subjects, add **-s** to the verb. If the subject is plural, the present-tense verb does not end in **-s.** Verbs used with the pronouns *I, you, we,* and *they* do not end in **s.**

> **Singular subject + verb** The ant <u>crawls</u> slowly.
> **Plural subject + verb** The ants <u>crawl</u> in a line.

A Complete each sentence with the correct form of the verb in ( ). Write the sentences.

1. The butterfly _____ a bright red flower. (see, sees)
2. It _____ on the flower's soft petals. (land, lands)
3. Butterflies _____ on pollen and nectar. (feed, feeds)
4. I _____ about their habits. (learn, learns)
5. They _____ like such gentle insects. (seem, seems)

Choose the words in ( ) that complete each sentence correctly. Write the sentences.

6. An (ant work, ant works) very hard.
7. The tiny (insect lift, insect lifts) big crumbs.
8. Some (ants become, ants becomes) soldiers.
9. (Army ants travel, Army ants travels) in a straight line.
10. The (worker ant serve, worker ant serves) the queen.
11. The (fire ant sting, fire ant stings) people.

B Write the sentence from each pair that is correct.

1. My favorite book tell all about lions.
   My favorite book tells all about lions.

2. They live in groups called prides.
   They lives in groups called prides.

3. Lions hunt for their food.
   Lions hunts for their food.

4. I learns many things from my books.
   I learn many things from my books.

C Write the correct form of the verb in ( ) to complete each sentence. Write the sentences.

5. Some animals (act) like humans.
6. Ants and bees (work) for a queen.
7. The mother bird (make) a soft nest for her eggs.
8. The father sea horse (raise) the baby sea horses.
9. Caged birds (look) at themselves in mirrors.
10. A dog's mood (change) sometimes.
11. Cats (need) calm places.

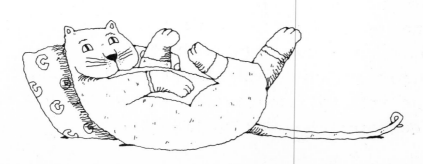

Review and Assess

Complete the sentences with the correct form of the verb in ( ).
Write the sentences.

1. I really _____ books of animal fables. (like, likes)
2. One story _____ a grasshopper and an ant. (compare, compares)
3. The ant _____ hard, unlike the grasshopper. (work, works)
4. Only the ant _____ enough food. (save, saves)

Write the letter of the verb that completes the sentence correctly.

5. My cat _____ the fish tank all day.

   A watching   **C** watches

   B were watching   **D** watch

6. Back and forth, one goldfish _____.

   A swims   **C** swim

   B swimming   **D** have swimmed

7. The cat _____ at the goldfish.

   A stares   **C** staring

   B stare   **D** is stare

8. They _____ this little game.

   A is liking   **C** likes

   B like   **D** liking

Using Verbs to Persuade

Use strong verbs to persuade your audience.

A Complete each sentence with a verb from the list, or use one of your own. Make sure subjects and verbs agree.

pounce   slither   visit   swoop   gnaws   learn

1. I think our class should _____ the zoo. **2.** We can _____ so much from the animals. **3.** Playful bear cubs _____ on one another. **4.** Bats _____ from the trees. **5.** Snakes _____ along the rocks. **6.** A hungry beaver _____ on a tree.

B Use strong verbs of your own to complete the sentences. Write the paragraph.

7. My cousin _____ when he sees my snakes. **8.** He saw three snakes _____ in the glass tank. **9.** He watched birds _____ in a cage. **10.** They always _____ loudly. **11.** How can I _____ him that pets are fun, not scary?

C Write a note persuading a family member to take you to the zoo. Remind the reader that you will learn many things at the zoo. Make subjects and verbs agree.

Writing a Persuasive Letter

A **test** may ask you to write a persuasive letter. When you choose your topic, think of reasons that will convince your reader. Use words such as *should* and *most important*. Follow the tips below.

Understand the prompt. Make sure you know what to do. Read the prompt carefully. A prompt for a persuasive letter could look like this:

> **Think of a place that you would like to visit. Then write a letter to your parents persuading them to vacation there.**

REASONS

You can state the best reason first or save it for last.

Key words are *letter, parents, persuading,* and *vacation.*

Find a good topic. Choose a place that you know details about and would like to visit.

Organize your ideas. Make a chart. Write your opening sentence. List supporting reasons. Star the best reason.

OPENING SENTENCE	SUPPORTING REASONS
I think we should spend part of July in Cape Cod.	Relax as a family * Friend goes there Bay and ocean Wide, clean beaches Hotels and camping grounds

Write a good beginning. State your main reason for writing the letter in the first sentence. Make your purpose clear.

Develop and elaborate ideas. Use the reasons from your chart. You can either begin or end with your strongest reason.

Write a strong ending. Try to make the ending convincing.

Check your work. Make any corrections that are needed.

See how the letter below addresses the prompt, has a strong beginning and end, and uses persuasive language.

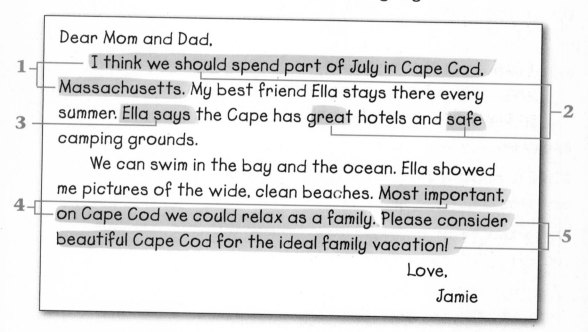

Dear Mom and Dad,

1 — I think we should spend part of July in Cape Cod, Massachusetts. My best friend Ella stays there every summer. Ella says the Cape has great hotels and safe — 2
3 — camping grounds.

We can swim in the bay and the ocean. Ella showed me pictures of the wide, clean beaches. Most important,
4 — on Cape Cod we could relax as a family. Please consider — 5
beautiful Cape Cod for the ideal family vacation!

Love,

Jamie

1. This first sentence states the reason for writing.
2. Language is persuasive and clear.
3. The subject and verb agree.
4. The most important reason comes last.
5. This ending makes a strong statement.

Art Acknowledgments

Franklin Hammond 7, 21, 22, 59, 64, 81, 92, 114, 128, 129, 135, 147

Rose Mary Berlin 30, 48, 60, 74, 95, 107, 113, 121, 132, 143